W9-BDD-091

The Council of Better Business Bureaus

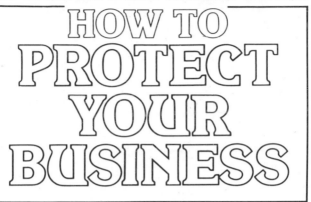

HOW TO
PROTECT
YOUR
BUSINESS

Published by

B

BENJAMIN

TO GET ADDITIONAL COPIES

Individual copies of this book are available from your local bookstore, local Better Business Bureau (addresses, Appendix B), or the Council of Better Business Bureaus, 1515 Wilson Boulevard, Arlington, VA 22209.

Special Discounts for Quantity Purchases

Special discounts for bulk quantities (100 and over) are offered to business firms, associations, government agencies, and other organizations that plan to use this book as a promotional, educational, or public relations tool. Back cover identification and message are available, subject to CBBB approval, on orders of 1,000 or more. Contact the publisher: The Benjamin Company, One Westchester Plaza, Elmsford, N.Y. 10523. Telephone: (914) 592-8088.

Research and Writing: **Neil William Sandler**

Editor: Virginia Schomp
Project Manager: Sara Woodard
Editorial Assistant: Annemarie Erena
Designer: Pam Forde Graphics
Illustrator: Ric Del Rossi / Mulvey Associates
Typography: Donnelley / Rocappi

Library of Congress Catalog Card Number: 85-070001
ISBN: 0-87502-143-3 Trade paperback, Benjamin Company edition
0-87502-144-1 Hardcover, Benjamin Company edition
0-87502-145-X Mass market paperback, Benjamin Company edition
0-13-430539-6 Trade paperback, Prentice-Hall edition
0-13-430547-7 Hardcover, Prentice-Hall edition

Produced and published by The Benjamin Company, Inc.
One Westchester Plaza
Elmsford, New York 10523

Fourth Printing: January 1988

*This book is dedicated to helping
the American business community
to fight those crimes that needlessly raise
the costs of goods and services
to its customers.*

Contents

One of the fastest growing, most lucrative industries in the U.S. during the next two decades will be crime against business. Illegal proceeds will exceed revenues earned in such high-tech fields as aero-space technology, computers, and bioengineering. While the rapidly escalating rate of crime against business has driven many companies out of business, an alert and educated businessperson is not defenseless.

The BBB Works With Business
You Are Not Defenseless
Figuratively Speaking
The Role of the BBB
How You Can Help

SECTION I
SCHEMES AGAINST BUSINESS

This rapidly growing multimillion-dollar-a-year scheme involves the unethical, but often legal, sale of poor quality, off-brand office supplies to businesses that think they are getting a name brand product at a special discount price.

The Case of the Careless Copier
Unethical, But Legal
"WATS-line Hustlers"
Protect Your Business
If You Are Victimized

Billing schemes typically prey on the inefficiency of business. Most cases involve the mailing of phony invoices to employees who are not careful enough in scrutinizing bills being processed for payment. Includes section on directory advertising fraud.

The Case of the Bogus Bill
Anatomy of a Scam
Solicitations in the Guise of Invoices
Directory Advertising Schemes
Protect Your Business
If You Are Victimized

American businesses are contacted regularly for donations to charities, foundations, and other worthy causes. Unfortunately, each year millions of dollars targeted toward worthy purposes are diverted into the pockets of swindlers.

While most organizations that lend money to businesses are legitimate, a growing number of self-proclaimed "loan brokers" offer to lend money they cannot provide—then abscond with the so-called "advance fees."

Taking advantage of recent changes in the law that are aimed at helping those with failed businesses get back on their feet, con artists and some formerly honest businesspeople are making a living by intentionally running businesses into the ground for profit.

"Once-in-a-lifetime" opportunities to invest in a business in which you are all but guaranteed to convert your investment of several thousand dollars into many times that amount are rare at best. In most cases, the only thing that really is guaranteed is a con artist willing and able to rid you of your investment capital.

SECTION II
EXTERNAL CRIME

Clothing designers aren't the only ones who earn a living by selling their name brand fashions. Unscrupulous manufacturers of clothing and other goods produce cheap imitations, then sell the low-quality merchandise to unwitting consumers as the "real thing." Both the original manufacturers and consumers lose out.

CHAPTER 8 **Crimes Practiced on Cashiers** 88

Quick-change artists, who confuse cashiers and walk away with more change than they originally paid, have been succeeded by more sophisticated schemers. The quick-change scheme is now joined by price tag and container switches and refund frauds, among others. Includes special section on counterfeit currency.

CHAPTER 9 **Shoplifting** 100

Professional and nonprofessional shoplifters have been known to steal just about any item for sale in a store. Keeping employees and managers alert for these culprits represents the first line of defense.

CHAPTER 10 **Credit Card Fraud** 108

As the dramatic increase in the use of credit cards almost replaces the use of cash for many Americans, great new horizons are drawn for criminals who find new ways to tap into this vast interchange of money. While stolen cards remain the primary avenue of crime, other schemes are catching up.

CHAPTER 11 **Check Fraud** 116

"Bounced" checks written against insufficient funds remain the most common problem, but businesses also must be alert to a variety of check fraud schemes.

SECTION III
INTERNAL CRIME

Preface

In recent years, crimes against business have become a growing force in this country, costing billions of dollars annually. These costs to business are inevitably passed on through the system to the consumer.

For more than 70 years, the Better Business Bureau system has been in the forefront of the battle to promote fair competition and protect consumers from dishonesty in the marketplace. With the support of ethical business, it has successfully promoted the concept that business self-regulation not only will alleviate the need for government intervention, but also will yield better returns than practices that deceive or defraud the public.

In keeping with its basic mission to protect the consumer and maintain an orderly marketplace, the Council of Better Business Bureaus and its affiliated Bureaus have joined together to produce this book. Its primary purpose is to help concerned businesses to combat the more common schemes that prey upon the unwary employee, manager, or owner.

In making the information contained herein available to the thousands of businesses that support the Bureau system, the Council hopes that it has contributed toward maintaining an orderly marketplace—to the benefit of buyer and seller alike.

William H. Tankersley
President
Council of Better Business Bureaus

Acknowledgments

Many individuals representing public and private agencies, organizations, and corporations contributed time and effort to this project. We gratefully acknowledge their assistance—the information they provided, their comments, criticisms, and suggestions. Their names are too numerous to mention, but special thanks must go to our friends at:

A. C. Nielsen Company
American Bankers Association
American Express Company
American Insurance Association
Audit Bureau of Circulations
Bank of America
Commodity Futures Trading Commission
Direct Marketing Association
District of Columbia Police Department
Federal Bureau of Investigation
Federal Trade Commission
Fraud and Theft Information Bureau
International Anticounterfeiting
    Coalition
Kentucky Department of Justice,
    Office of Crime Prevention
MasterCard
National Computer Association
National Freight Claim Council of
    the American Trucking Associations
National Retail Merchants Association
U.S. Attorney General's Office
U.S. Chamber of Commerce
U.S. Commissioner of Patents and
    Trademarks
U.S. Department of Commerce
U.S. Department of Justice
U.S. Postal Service
U.S. Secret Service
U.S. Small Business Administration
VISA International
    and
Retail Consultants: Richard Bigness
                    Jon Groetzinger

Introduction

One of the fastest growing, most lucrative industries in America today is crime against business.

Through the 1980s and 1990s, the dollar value of cash, merchandise, and information obtained through employee theft, computer fraud, office supply schemes, bribes, kickbacks, credit card fraud, and related crimes will far outpace that earned in such highly touted, high-tech industries as aerospace, computers, and bioengineering. Surprisingly, knowledgeable crime watchers predict that for the most part this accelerating crime wave will comprise not such familiar, well-publicized crimes as robbery and shoplifting, but rather "white-collar" crimes and a whole new class of schemes and frauds perpetrated both within and outside targeted businesses.

Consider the following facts:

- In the early 1980s, an average of 20,000 credit card crimes are committed *every day,* according to the Committee on Banking, Finance and Urban Affairs of the U.S. Congress.

- Foreign product counterfeiting was responsible for the loss of over 130,000 U.S. jobs in 1982, reports the International Trade Commission.

- One-fifth of the investigative staff of the Federal Bureau of Investigation (FBI) in 1982 was targeted exclusively at detecting fraud and white-collar crime. The result: nearly 4,000 convictions and an estimated $2.6 billion in crime prevented.

- The combined losses due to shoplifting and internal pilferage by employees add up to 15 percent of retail prices, estimates the U.S. Department of Commerce.

- The National Office Products Association cites annual losses of $50 million to businesses due to office supply schemes, but notes the actual figure may be even higher.

- In the bank credit card industry alone, losses due to the fraudulent use of credit cards rose from about $11 million in 1972 to over $125 million a decade later—over a 1,000 percent increase.

- Computer crimes perpetrated in a scant 0.0003 second (3 milliseconds) have netted these specialized criminals millions of dollars.

- Insurance fraud results in annual losses of $4 billion, a figure reported to be spiraling upward.

- White-collar crime losses total $40 billion a year, reports the FBI.

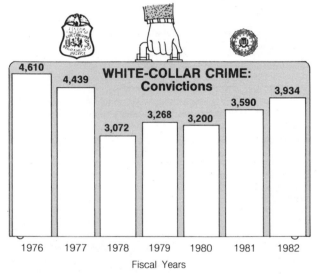

WHITE-COLLAR CRIME: Convictions

1976	1977	1978	1979	1980	1981	1982
4,610	4,439	3,072	3,268	3,200	3,590	3,934

Fiscal Years

Prepared by U.S. Department of Justice, Federal Bureau of Investigation

The BBB Works with Business

During more than 70 years of operation, the Council of Better Business Bureaus and its network of local BBBs have documented thousands of cases in which businesses have suffered at the hands of con artists and schemers. The victims include a wide variety of businesses, from neighborhood "mom and pop" stores to multi-national conglomerates.

13

You Are Not Defenseless

The stereotypical armed bandit is becoming of almost secondary concern as, increasingly, culprits turn out to be trusted employees, family members, or friends. This phenomenon demands a whole new manner of vigilance.

A little knowledge is a very useful thing when it comes to recognizing and foiling a fraud, scheme, or theft. While there are no foolproof solutions to the serious crime problems discussed in this book, you can keep losses to a minimum by knowing and applying these four basic principles.

- Be aware of your crime losses.

- Apply risk management techniques to prevent crimes before they occur.

- Train employees at all levels in crime prevention.

- Report all illegal activities to the appropriate law enforcement authorities.

This book describes how various schemes work, how you can defend your business against con artists and schemers, and what legal recourses to use if you are victimized. Although there are areas in which the nature of operation of the various types of schemes overlaps, we have divided the white-collar crimes commonly committed against business into three categories. Section I deals with "Schemes Against Business," including office supply schemes, phony invoice schemes, charity schemes, loan broker fraud, bankruptcy fraud, and business opportunity schemes. Section II, "External Crime," covers product counterfeiting, crimes practiced on cashiers, shoplifting, credit card fraud, check fraud, coupon fraud, and cargo theft. Section III addresses some of the fastest growing and most damaging types of business crimes—"Internal Crime." This section covers embezzlement and pilferage; bribery, kickbacks, and payoffs; insurance fraud; and computer crimes.

A book could be written on each of the topics covered. But we feel that it is most important for every businessperson to acquire a basic understanding of the most prevalent forms of the crimes that threaten their businesses. That knowledge is the first important step in learning how to stop, or at least reduce the risk of, crime against business.

Figuratively Speaking

In an effort to indicate the extent of losses sustained by the business community due to crimes directed against it, we have contacted numerous government agencies, business organizations and associations, law enforcement officials, and private monitoring groups. Nearly all of these groups caution that it is virtually impossible to compile totally accurate statistics in this area, the main barrier being the frequent non-reportage of crimes against business. The National Institute of Justice points out that some businesspeople who become aware that they are victims of such crimes as internal theft and fraud resolve these problems internally, never making their losses public; others write them off as an inevitable cost of doing business. Embarrassment also may discourage the reporting of crimes to public agencies or business groups. And, of course, there are the crimes that are never detected, often because businesspeople have not been trained to recognize the tell-tale signs. For whatever reason, many crimes against business never become part of official estimates, making many statistics little more than educated guesses. The figures we cite constitute the "best guesses" of a host of individuals and organizations, but the reader should be aware that even among the experts, figures often vary widely.

The Role of the BBB

Our goal is to help you avoid becoming a victim of the kinds of crime covered in this book. A special section in each chapter details your legal recourses and the appropriate agencies to contact if you *are* victimized, and Appendix A provides addresses and phone numbers for the agencies cited.

We urge you also to contact your local Better Business Bureau. Appendix B provides addresses and phone numbers for the 165 local BBBs in the U.S.

Local Bureaus assist businesses and consumers through:

☐ Pertinent information. Each local Bureau keeps files on large numbers of firms and organizations in its service area. BBBs provide such basic information as how long a firm has been in business, whether or not customers or other businesses have filed complaints, and the nature of complaints and the manner in which the firm resolved them. BBBs can also provide factual information on local and national charitable organizations. We provide the facts; you draw your own conclusions.

☐ Complaint handling. Acting as impartial third parties, BBBs actively work for mutually acceptable solutions to disputes between businesses, and between consumers and businesses.

☐ Checks on advertising claims. BBBs regularly monitor advertisements and investigate misleading or inaccurate claims. In addition, the Bureaus handle complaints from businesses concerning competitors' advertising.

☐ Standards development. Working with industry and business groups, the BBB develops voluntary advertising codes and standards.

How You Can Help

We hope that readers will bring to our attention schemes against business that are not covered in this book, as well as unusual variations of the crimes outlined in these pages. Only by working with you can we continue to assist you and your business colleagues in combatting our common enemy, crime against business. Please direct your comments to:

Public Information Department
Council of Better Business Bureaus
1515 Wilson Boulevard
Arlington, VA 22209

SECTION I

SCHEMES
AGAINST
BUSINESS

CHAPTER 1

THE CASE OF

The Careless Copier

A call comes into a small business office from a representative of its "regular supplier of office products" and is passed along to the employee who operates the photocopier. The caller—ostensibly in order to "update her files"—requests verification of the make and model number of the company's photocopier and then explains that her records indicate it is time for the company to reorder supplies. Since shipments normally take a few weeks, she recommends the order be placed now. Lulled by the caller's smooth, matter-of-fact manner, the employee approves the order.

Several weeks later, the supplies arrive, directed to the attention of the employee who approved the order and who now approves the shipment by signing a delivery form. The subsequent invoice is also okayed by the employee, who assures the accounting department that the supplies have been received. The bill is promptly paid and the supplies are placed in storage.

Office Supply Schemes and "Paper Pirates"

During a periodic maintenance call, a technician from the manufacturer of the machine notices the boxes of photocopier supplies and sternly informs the office manager that the use of these "off-brand" supplies could harm the equipment and invalidate the company's warranty. A look at the records reveals that the company has never before done business with this "off-brand" supplier, and when the office manager tries to return the supplies for a refund, the supply company responds that returns are against its policy. Besides, the delivery form, signed by a company employee, clearly states, "All sales final."

Unethical, But Legal

Every year, millions of dollars' worth of high-quality, fairly priced office supplies are sold over the telephone by honest, reputable suppliers. Unfortunately for many businesses and organizations, millions of dollars are also conned out of U.S. businesses each year by office supply schemers and ''paper pirates'' like the one described above. The National Office Products Association estimates annual business losses at $50 million but notes that figures could actually be much higher; the large majority of these rip-offs go either undetected or unreported because the supplies are used or the victims embarrassed to acknowledge they've been ''taken.''

Even when the victim is aware of the swindle, in many cases there is no legal recourse. While their schemes might be highly unethical, the perpetrators usually devise them in a manner that is totally legal. Telephone salespeople for these unethical operations are carefully trained not to misrepresent their employers, and their meticulously scripted ''pitches'' avoid identifying their operations with brand name suppliers or manufacturers.

This is not to say that swindlers can't mislead the hapless target on the other end of the telephone by, for example, offering to sell photocopier toner ''for your ABC copier''—not at all the same thing as ''ABC toner.'' Some hustlers also package their off-brand supplies to look like brand name products.

''WATS-line Hustlers''

Paper-pirate and office supply schemes frequently operate from ramshackle supply warehouses thousands of miles from their prospective victims. For their use of long-distance telephone lines, such as the Wide Area Telecommunications Service, or WATS line, these solicitors have been dubbed ''WATS-line hustlers'' by law enforcement officials.

According to the Federal Trade Commission (FTC), typical WATS-line hustlers target all kinds of businesses and organizations, including restaurants, professional offices, religious groups, schools, and hospitals. They generally sell products needing constant replacement, such as office supplies (pens, typewriter ribbons, photocopier paper, ink, or toner) and maintenance supplies (light bulbs, cleaning compounds).

The telephone solicitors often read from printed scripts and use a printed list of responses to deflect objections.

While WATS-line hustlers use many different ploys, the FTC identifies the following common tactics.

☐ **They rarely deal with the authorized purchasing agent.** WATS-line hustlers usually try to talk with an employee who is unfamiliar with purchasing procedures; e.g., an inexperienced clerk, secretary, or maintenance person. They may use the name of the authorized purchasing agent or of another employee to convince the unwitting victim to divulge information or approve an order.

☐ **They may mislead you to solicit an order.** WATS-line hustlers usually try to mislead you into believing that they represent your regular supplier. The National Office Products Association cautions that one of the most recent and effective scams involves the fraudulent use of the name of a business's actual supplier to solicit orders. Hustlers also have been known to introduce themselves as representing a storage company with an impressive-sounding name like Central Disbursement or the Central Warehouse.

☐ **They might try to con you with a fabricated tale of a "disaster"** that allows them to offer substantial savings by selling supplies at sharply reduced prices. Overturned tractor-trailers, fire sales, and liquidations are among the many fictions used.

☐ **They may claim to be conducting a survey of office equipment or updating their records.** Once you have given them the information they need (for example, the model number on your photocopier), they may pose as your new supplier or as authorized dealer for the products you use.

☐ **They may try to pressure you into placing an immediate order.** WATS-line hustlers may offer "bargain prices" if you order right away—but their prices are usually no bargain. The pitch that prices are "going up tomorrow" or that, since you mistakenly were not notified of a price increase, you are entitled to a special "one-time-only" purchase at the "old" price, is aimed at pushing you into immediate, imprudent action.

☐ **They may offer free gifts.** To induce you to place an order, WATS-line hustlers may offer to send a free personal gift, such as a transistor radio or calculator, to your home. Most likely, the gift will never arrive, and even if it does, its value will rarely be offset by the inflated price of the products ordered.

☐ **They may misrepresent merchandise,** including the quality, type, size, and brand of their products.

☐ **They may refuse to accept returned merchandise.** If you complain about the products received, WATS-line hustlers may try to persuade you to keep the shipment at a so-called "discount price." They usually refuse to accept returned merchandise or pay for return shipments, and may attempt to charge you for storage or damages.

PROTECT YOUR BUSINESS

Because there are so many variations of the paper-pirate and office supply swindles, it would be almost impossible to anticipate and guard against every possible approach. But there are steps you can take to keep your company from being victimized.

1. Never buy from a new supplier by telephone or mail until you have verified its existence and reliability. Ask for references and check them, find out how long the firm has operated out of its present location (and, if possible, visit the company), and ask your local BBB for a report.

2. Do not accept Cash on Delivery (COD) shipments. Insist on open account billing; that way, if there's a problem, you have some leverage.

3. Insist on sending written purchase orders.

4. Designate purchasing agents for ordering, receiving, and paying for supplies.

5. Inform all employees about your organization's purchasing, receiving, and payment systems. Alert employees to the office supply racket and to the inadvisability of giving out information on makes and models of office equipment over the phone.

IF YOU ARE VICTIMIZED

If you think you have been the victim of a paper-pirate or office supply scheme, the Better Business Bureau recommends that you first
contact the supplier and attempt to work out an amicable solution. If
the supplier is uncooperative, your next step will depend on the stage
at which you become aware of the scheme.

Unpaid-for Merchandise

If you have not paid for the merchandise and you feel that it has been
misrepresented, withhold payment and do not use the merchandise.
Then take the following steps.

1. Send a certified letter to the company explaining your position
   and how you expect the company to settle the matter, e.g., by
   taking back the merchandise.

2. If the firms fails to respond within your stated period of time,
   send a copy of your letter to your local Better Business Bureau,
   with a cover letter asking the BBB for assistance.

3. If the problem remains unresolved, notify your local police department and the nearest office of the FTC. If the U.S. mail has
   been used in any way by the organization attempting to defraud
   you, contact the Chief Postal Inspector, U.S. Postal Service
   (See Appendix A).

4. If at this stage the supplier threatens to take legal action or to
   turn your account over to a collection agency, contact an attorney and your state attorney general's office, listed under state
   government in most telephone directories.

Unordered Merchandise Sent By U.S. Mail

1. Under federal law, you are entitled to regard unordered merchandise sent through the U.S. mail as a free gift. The same law makes it illegal to mail bills for such unordered merchandise. Note, however, that this does not include merchandise sent in error.

2. You can refuse a shipment arriving by U.S. mail if you don't open it. To avoid misunderstandings, first send the company shipping the merchandise a letter (preferably certified with a return receipt requested) asking for proof of your order.

3. If you are positive the merchandise was not ordered, write the shipper that you are keeping it as a free gift and sending a copy of your letter to the FTC. Keep copies of all correspondence for your records.

Unordered Merchandise Sent By Private Delivery Services

1. If unordered merchandise arrives by private delivery, do not accept the shipment.

2. If you have already accepted the shipment, send the shipper a certified letter, return receipt requested, demanding proof of your order. If there is no valid proof, inform the sender that unless the merchandise is picked up within 30 days, you will dispose of it. By giving the sender an opportunity to recover the merchandise, you invalidate any claim that you accepted an offer of sale merely by keeping the shipment.

3. If you return the merchandise, do so at the sender's expense and get a receipt from the carrier.

4. If an invoice for the unordered merchandise arrives, withhold payment and do not use the merchandise. If the firm fails to respond to your letter, contact your local Better Business Bureau for assistance.

5. If the BBB cannot help you resolve the problem, notify your local police department and the nearest office of the FTC.

6. If the supplier threatens you with legal action, contact an attorney and your state attorney general's office, listed under state government in most telephone directories.

When They Insist You Placed an Order

1. WATS-line hustlers often insist that an order was placed and verified. Before you accept or pay for any merchandise that arrives under less-than-clear circumstances, protect yourself by insisting on proof that an order was placed. If no proof is forthcoming, follow the appropriate steps listed above.

2. If you believe the sender made an honest mistake, you can offer to return the goods at the sender's expense.

3. If it turns out that a verifiable order was placed and you have received exactly what was ordered, you are responsible for paying the bill.

CHAPTER 2

THE CASE OF

The Bogus Bill

The head of maintenance for a large chain of department stores receives a call from "the governor's energy office." As part of an "official survey" of the state's most energy efficient businesses, the caller would like to ask some questions about the department store chain's efforts to reduce energy consumption.

The maintenance chief is flattered to receive a call from a high-level official. Proudly, he describes his company's conscientious efforts, including a new program of phasing in energy efficient light bulbs. The caller's respectful inquiries elicit all the details: when bulbs are replaced, how many, what type, at what cost.

Several weeks later, shortly after the chain has completed its most recent bulb replacement, the accounting department receives a $2,200 invoice for light bulbs. The bill contains all the correct details of the company's normal quarterly supply, including the name of the head of maintenance as originator of the order.

Phony Invoice Schemes

With everything appearing to be in order, the bill is processed through accounting and paid. It isn't until two weeks later, when a second bill for exactly the same purchase arrives, that some serious questions are raised. Accounting discovers, much to its chagrin, that while this new bill is legitimate, the first was not. To make matters worse, the check sent in payment of the first invoice has been cashed. And the firm is no longer at the listed address.

Anatomy of a Scam

Phony invoicing schemes, of which the above story is one example, typically prey on the inefficiency of targeted businesses. For their successful execution, these schemes rely on sloppy bookkeeping, inattention on the part of employees, and perhaps most importantly, the failure of one arm of a business to know what the other arm is doing.

The U.S. Postal Service contends that con artists succeed in collecting a significant percentage of all the bills they mail, but notes that due to the nature of the crime, it is impossible to determine the exact extent of losses. While law enforcement officials are unable to place an actual dollar figure on the amount swindled each year, the fact that this type of swindler mails thousands of phony invoices and solicitations disguised as invoices on a regular basis points to an annual loss to businesses that may run into billions of dollars.

While there is no set formula for these invoice schemes, most involve the use of an initial telephone contact. The call helps the swindler obtain the names of key business contacts as well as some important details about the operation of the business and its products or services.

The persons making these calls are, for the most part, remarkably smooth operators. Often brazen and forward in their approaches, they have been known to talk their way through a chain of receptionists, secretaries, assistant managers, supervisors, and vice presidents to gain access to heads of companies. In most cases, however, they need gain access to only lower-level employees.

The con artist's next contact with the intended victim commonly comes in the form of a phony invoice sent through the mail. The invoice, which includes names, figures, and other details that add to the appearance of legitimacy, may be paid unwittingly along with a number of other routine bills. In many cases, the amount of the invoice is just small enough to slip by the checkwriter's attention. The swindler has had considerable experience calculating the most effective dollar amount, depending on variables such as the size of the firm and the control it seems to have on its management system. Thousands of mass-mailed invoices, each for just a few dollars, may prove more lucrative than several large invoices.

"Scare tactics" sometimes are used to increase the odds of success. A phony invoice or past-due notice stamped "Pay This Bill Now" or "We Are About to Start Action" may intimidate the victim into rushing to make out a check without carefully investigating the supposedly delinquent charge.

Individuals also may be victimized by phony invoice schemes, through fraudulent invoices mailed to their homes. And to compound the injury, beleaguered victims, whether individuals or businesses, are quickly identified once they pay and are often flooded with additional invoices for nonexistent subscriptions, supplies, and services.

Solicitations in the Guise of Invoices

One of the most common variations of the phony invoice scheme is solicitations disguised as invoices. These documents, which actually are solicitations for the purchase of goods or services, are carefully designed to look like legitimate invoices for goods or services ordered and received. In some cases, the small print may identify the bogus bill as a solicitation. The business that pays a solicitation disguised as an invoice may receive the merchandise or service it was duped into ordering; more often, it will not, and efforts to trace the fraudulent firm that issued the "invoice" will prove futile.

The deceptive solicitation may be received through the mail or may be presented in person by an "advertising salesperson" who visits a business office on the pretext of saving company handling charges. The invoice may be accompanied by fabricated proof of the ad's placement, with the con artist clipping an actual company ad and reproducing it in a spurious edition of a nonexistent publication.

Most of these schemes involve the issuing of an invoice for an advertisement in a publication, journal, or directory targeted at a particular ethnic or special-interest group. The directory or its circulation may not be at all as implied or described; quite often, the publication does not exist.

We Are Now About To Start Action

DIRECTED TO THE ATTENTION OF

AUTHORIZED

USE ENCLOSED ENVELOPE FOR YOUR CHECK TO PAY THIS BILL NOW

THEME ISSUE
VETERANS

SPECIAL COPY CONTENTS
YEARBOOK VETERANS SALUTE   AMOUNT DUE 89.20

MAILING ADDRESS

FILE COPY

31

Directory Advertising Schemes

Most, but not all, directory advertising schemes involve the issuing of solicitations disguised as invoices. Other displays of the con artist's skill in the exploitation of inefficiency and emotions include the following variations.

- A bogus "advertising salesperson" calls or visits an office to ask if a business wishes to renew an ad allegedly placed "last year." The caller makes the transaction sound routine, and the business agrees to continue running the ad. An invoice is received—perhaps supported by a trumped-up "clipping"—and is paid. Frequently, the publication doesn't exist.

- A con artist manipulates embarrassment or emotions to sell an ad in a worthless or nonexistent ethnic-oriented publication.

- A businessperson, fearful of appearing uncooperative, is pressured into placing an ad in a law enforcement publication.

 PROTECT YOUR BUSINESS

The best protection against invoice frauds or schemes is knowledge and vigilance. Your company's accounting department or the persons responsible for paying bills should be made aware of the fake bill racket and should watch out for solicitations disguised as invoices and for dubious bills from unfamiliar companies.

Specifically, observe the following precautions.

1. Never place an order over the telephone unless there is no doubt that the firm you are dealing with is reputable. Get the organization's name, address, and phone number, as well as its representative's full name and position. If a significant amount of money is involved, ask for business references and references with local banks and check them. Find out how long the firm has operated out of its present location (and, if possible, visit the company), and ask your local Better Business Bureau for a report.

2. Check your records to confirm claims of previous business dealings.

3. Before placing advertising, verify that the publication exists and that its circulation suits your needs. Circulation figures can be verified by contacting the Audit Bureau of Circulations (See Appendix A).

4. Establish effective internal controls for the payment of invoices.

   - Channel all bills through one department.

   - Insist that employees fill out prenumbered purchase orders for every order placed.

   - Check all invoices against purchase orders and against goods or services received. Make certain that order numbers correspond.

   - Verify all invoices with the person who gave written or verbal authorization.

   - Clear all invoices with the appropriate executives.

   - Insist on hearing a tape recording of the order if the invoicing company claims to have one.

Know the Law

The law is clear-cut and specific in its position on solicitations. It is against U.S. Postal Service regulations to mail a bill, invoice, or statement of account due that is actually a solicitation, unless it bears one of the following disclaimers.

> *This is a solicitation for the order of goods or services, or both, and not a bill, invoice, or statement of account due. You are under no obligation to make any payments on account of this offer unless you accept this offer.*

OR

> *This is not a bill. This is a solicitation. You are under no obligation to pay unless you accept this offer.*

One of these disclaimers must be conspicuously printed on the face of the solicitation in at least 30-point type. That is type

Print colors must be reproducible on copying machines and cannot be obscured by folding or other means. If the solicitation is more than one page, the disclaimer must appear on each page, and if it is perforated, the required language must appear on each section which could be construed as a bill. Regulations prohibit any language that modifies or qualifies the disclaimer, such as "legal notice required by law." Mailing solicitations that do not meet these requirements can result in a U.S. Postal Service stop order under which responses are returned to the sender, cutting off the soliciting firm's source of revenue.

Other forms of phony invoice schemes may involve mail fraud or may violate other federal postal regulations.

 # IF YOU ARE VICTIMIZED

If you receive a phony invoice or a solicitation disguised as an invoice, use the following procedure to report the matter to the U.S. Postal Service and your local Better Business Bureau.

1. On the envelope in which the phony invoice or solicitation arrived, note the date received and sign your name. Be sure all the solicitation material is returned to the envelope in which it was received.

2. Prepare a notarized affidavit per the following sample.

3. Send the solicitation material and the original affidavit to the Chief Postal Inspector, U.S. Postal Service. Keep a copy for your records, and send a copy to your local Better Business Bureau (See Appendix B).

If you become aware of the scheme only after payments have been made on the fraudulent invoices, immediately contact the Chief Postal Inspector, your local police department, and the BBB. In most cases, you will be instructed to stop payment on your check or money order. The postal authorities should also inform you if any recourse is possible. If potential losses are considerable, contact your attorney for help in expediting your case.

TO: Chief Postal Inspector
     Attn: Fraud Section
     United States Postal Service
     Washington, D.C. 20260

Affidavit

I, _____

being duly sworn, depose and say:

1. I am _____ of _____
        (position)   (company)
   located at _____ .
              (address and zip code)

2. On or about _____ our firm received
                  (date)
   through the United States mail a solicitation from
   _____
   _____
                 (name and address)
   which resembles a bill, invoice, or statement of account.

3. I have dated and signed the solicitation material and
   enclosed it herewith.

4. Our firm has never done business with _____
   _____
                      (name)
   and we have not requested a listing or authorized the
   insertion of our advertisement in the publication referred to in the solicitation.

5. It is my opinion that the subject solicitation represents
   an attempt to elicit a remittance from my firm by means
   of deception.

                    _____
                              (signature)

Subscribed and sworn to before me this _____ day of

_____, _____

My commission expires _____ .

CHAPTER 3

A CASE OF

Misguided Generosity

A well-dressed man introducing himself as a representative of a non-profit organization that helps families in need visits a corporate office. Meeting with a company executive, the man discusses the specific needs of the families his organization assists. He hands the executive a glossy brochure with pictures of the families and graphic descriptions of their privations. Also included in the brochure is a chart showing the amounts of money considered "fair" contributions from companies of varying sizes.

The "Charity" Plea

After conferring with "higher ups," the executive agrees to donate a company check for the requested amount. The executive and other company officials are satisfied that their business has done its part to help the needy families in its community. What they don't know is that less than ten percent of their contribution will actually help families in need. The remainder will go toward paying high salaries for the fund raisers and extravagant overhead charges for the organization.

$3 Billion Annually

American businesses regularly are asked for donations to worthy causes. According to the American Association of Fund Raising Counsel, $3.1 billion in money and merchandise was contributed to charitable causes by American corporations in 1983, and the amount is increasing annually. It is impossible to say how much of this goes to support the cause as the contributor intended.

While a cautious examination of charitable appeals clearly is in order, many people find it difficult to refuse a request for help. Some businesspeople are sensitive to the needs of the community; others are afraid of appearing cold-blooded by turning down a request; some even fear neighborhood resistance or boycotts from their customers—the very people upon whom they depend for their livelihood.

Despite such concerns, careful evaluation of charitable solicitations—and rejection of those pleas that fail to meet standards—is not only smart business practice, but is one of the responsibilities of the community-minded business. Deceptive charity pleas defraud businesses and consumers and injure legitimate, more cost-effective and responsible charitable groups by undermining their efforts to raise funds for truly worthwhile causes.

PROTECT YOUR BUSINESS

The most effective way a business or individual can have a positive impact on society through charitable giving is by becoming a well-informed giver. When you consider contributions of your or your employer's money, merchandise, name, or time, make sure the donation will serve the purpose you intend.

Organizations that approach businesses or the public for charitable contributions should provide, upon request, all the information that a potential donor might reasonably wish to consider. In its close and extensive contacts with legitimate charitable organizations, the Better Business Bureau has found that responsible groups are more than willing to provide such information.

You usually can obtain reliable information by requesting and reviewing a copy of the charity's complete annual report and financial statements.

These reports should provide:

1. The full name and permanent address of the organization.

PHILANTHROPY IN 1983
(in billions of dollars)
[Total Contributions: $64.93 billion]

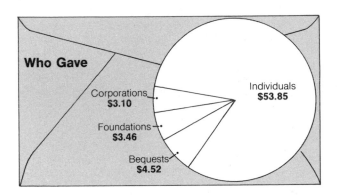

Who Gave

Corporations
$3.10

Foundations
$3.46

Bequests
$4.52

Individuals
$53.85

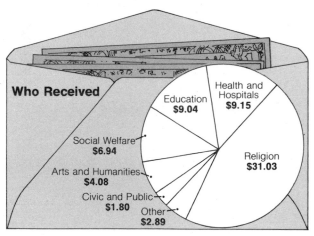

Who Received

Education
$9.04

Health and
Hospitals
$9.15

Social Welfare
$6.94

Arts and Humanities
$4.08

Civic and Public
$1.80

Other
$2.89

Religion
$31.03

Source: American Association of Fund Raising Counsel, Inc.

2. A clear description of the organization's purposes.

3. Descriptions of programs and activities.

4. A list of accomplishments.

5. Information about the governing body and its structure.

6. Details of management and staff responsibilities and services.

7. An elaboration on its legal eligibility to receive tax deductible contributions. (Keep in mind that "tax exempt" is not the same as "tax deductible." See pages 40 to 44.)

8. Information about financial activities, such as income, fund raising costs, and financial position.

Examine the financial information provided by the organization to be certain that the statements have been audited in accordance with generally accepted accounting principles. Other specifics to look for include: a breakdown of expenses into categories of programs, fund raising, and management; a detailed schedule of expenses, such as salaries, employee benefits, travel expenses, and mailing; and notes about business transactions with board members. In particular, determine approximately what percentage of public contributions are applied to the programs and activities described in the solicitation.

The Better Business Bureau recommends that at least 50 percent of a charity's total income from all sources be spent on programs and activities directly related to the organization's purposes. In addition, fund raising costs should not exceed 35 percent of related contributions. In applying these guidelines, however, donors should consider extenuating circumstances, such as unusual bequests, donor restrictions on the use of funds, and the unique expenses of a newly founded organization.

Donors should also be wary of excessive pressure applied by the fund raiser. Threats of public exposure, economic retaliation, and strongly worded emotional appeals should raise a warning flag.

□ ═══════════════════════════════════════ □

TAX EXEMPT VS. TAX DEDUCTIBLE

"Tax exempt" does not necessarily mean "tax deductible." A tax exempt organization is one that does not have to pay taxes; a tax deductible organization is one that is eligible to receive donations which may be deducted on the donor's federal income tax return. While the Internal Revenue Service defines more than twenty different categories of tax exempt organizations, only a few of these categories are also tax deductible.

You can determine the tax status of an organization either by contacting the local office of the Internal Revenue Service or by asking the organization for a copy of its IRS "Letter of Determination." A "Letter of Determination" is the formal notification an organization receives from the IRS once its tax status has been approved.

Soliciting organizations generally fall into the following three tax exempt categories: 501(c)(3), 501(c)(4), and 501(c)(6). The principal tax deductible grouping is the 501(c)(3) category, broadly termed "charitable organizations."

501(c)(3)

To obtain a 501(c)(3) status, a nonprofit organization must file documents with the IRS that prove it to be operated for certain charitable purposes specified by the IRS. (Older charities may have a 101(6) ruling, which corresponds to section 501(c)(3) of the 1954 Code.)

Organizations in the 501(c)(3) category include groups whose purposes are:

- Charitable
- Religious
- Scientific
- Educational
- Literary
- Preventing cruelty to children or animals
- Fostering national or international amateur sports competition (if athletic facilities and equipment are not provided)
- Testing for public safety

Contributions to all 501(c)(3) organizations, with the single exception of the "testing for public safety" category, are deductible as charitable donations for federal income tax purposes.

Foundation Status

While its 501(c)(3) status determines that an organization is eligible to receive tax deductible donations, its foundation status determines the limits of an individual donor's deduction.

The three principal foundation status categories are as follows:

A public charity (identified in IRS terms as "not a private foundation") normally receives a substantial part of its income, directly or indirectly, from the general public or from the government. The public support must be fairly broad, not limited to a few individuals or families. [Public charities are defined in the Internal Revenue Code under section 509(a)(1).]

A private foundation, sometimes called a nonoperating foundation, receives most of its income from investments and endowments. This income is used to make grants to other organizations, rather than disbursed directly for charitable activities. [Private foundations are defined in the Internal Revenue Code under section 509(a).]

A private operating foundation is one which, although lacking general public support, devotes most of its earnings and assets directly to the conduct of its tax exempt purposes, rather than making grants to other organizations for these purposes. [Private operating foundations are defined in the Internal Revenue Code under section 4942(j)(3).]

Deductibility Limitations to 501(c)(3) Groups

Individuals giving to 501(c)(3) organizations that are either public charities or private operating foundations may deduct contributions representing up to 50 percent of the donor's adjusted gross income.

Individuals giving to 501(c)(3) organizations that are private foundations may deduct contributions representing up to 20 percent of their adjusted gross income. *Corporations* may deduct all contributions to 501(c)(3) organizations (regardless of foundation status), up to an amount equal to 10 percent of their pretax net income.

501(c)(4)

This group includes civic leagues, social welfare organizations, and local associations of employees. According to the IRS, "social welfare organizations" include such groups as volunteer fire departments and civic associations. Organizations that perform a substantial amount of legislative lobbying in behalf of specific issues are often classified as 501(c)(4). (See "Lobbying Restrictions for Tax Exempt Organizations," below.)

Lobbying Restrictions for Tax Exempt Organizations

There is no limitation on the extent to which 501(c)(4) and 501(c)(6) organizations may lobby for or against legislation. However, lobbying may not be a "substantial" part of the activities of a 501(c)(3) organization. Permissible levels of lobbying activity are clearly specified for 501(c)(3) groups which elect to come under the alternative lobbying criteria of the Tax Reform Act of 1976.

Contributions to 501(c)(4) organizations are not deductible as charitable donations but may be deductible as a business expense.
There are two exceptions to this rule:

- Contributions to volunteer fire companies and similar organizations, if used for public purposes.

- Contributions to most war veterans' organizations. (Note: Although a new category has been created for them, some veterans' organizations may still have a 501(c)(4) ruling.)

Contributions to these two types of 501(c)(4) organizations are deductible as charitable donations.

501(c)(6)

Nonprofit organizations ruled tax exempt under section 501(c)(6) include business leagues, chambers of commerce, real estate boards, and boards of trade. *Contributions to 501(c)(6) organizations are not deductible as charitable donations for federal income tax purposes. Donations may be deducted as a business expense if "ordinary and necessary" in the conduct of the taxpayer's business.*

501(c)(19)

A newly created category for veterans' organizations is the 501(c)(19) classification. *Contributions to some 501(c)(19) organizations may be deductible as charitable donations for federal income tax purposes.* (Those veterans' organizations that still have a 501(c)(4) ruling may also be eligible to receive contributions deductible as charitable donations.)

Other Tax Deductible Contributions

In addition to the 501(c)(3), 501(c)(19), and specific 501(c)(4) organizations previously named, the following tax exempt groups are eligible to receive tax deductible contributions.

- Cooperative hospital associations—[501(e)]

- Cooperative service organizations of operating educational organizations—[501(f)]

- Nonprofit cemetery companies—[501(c)(13)], if given for care of the cemetery as a whole rather than for a particular plot.

- Domestic fraternal societies and associations [501(c)(10)] and fraternal beneficiary societies and associations [501(c)(8)], if the contributions are used for charitable [that is, 501(c)(3)] purposes.

- Corporations organized and tax exempt under an Act of Congress which serve as instrumentalities of the U.S. [501(c)(1)]. Examples include the Reconstruction Finance Corporation, Federal Reserve Banks, and Federal Credit Unions.

When Can You Deduct?

1. Contributions are deductible for the year in which they are actually paid or unconditionally delivered, as by mail. Pledges are not deductible until the year paid.

2. The value of volunteer time or services to a charitable organization is not deductible.

3. Out-of-pocket expenses directly related to voluntary services to a charitable organization are deductible.

4. Contributions for which the donor receives a gift or benefits are deductible *only* to the extent that the donation exceeds the value of any consideration or benefit received by the donor. Dues, for example, may merely cover the cost of benefits received by the donor and are therefore not deductible; or they may be called dues but actually constitute a contribution for which the donor receives little or no benefit or monetary value in return. The cost of the benefit and/or the amount in excess of costs should be disclosed by the charitable organization.

5. Direct contributions to needy individuals are not deductible. The contributions must be to qualified organizations.

6. Contributions made directly to a foreign organization are not deductible, except in the case of some Canadian and Honduran organizations as specified in agreements with those countries.

7. Donated property may generally be deducted at the fair market value of the property at the time of the contribution. However, appreciated property is subject to special rules.

□ ═══ □

Your Good Name

Contributing money is only one of the ways in which you and your business may be asked to assist charitable groups. Other common approaches include requests that you serve as sponsor or nominal head of a fund raising drive, give your time as a volunteer or neighborhood solicitor, or serve on the board of a charitable organization.

When you allow your name or your company's name to be used by an organization, it is assumed that you also are lending your active support to its activities and fund raising procedures. Your reputation is on the line. Therefore, it is doubly important that you secure detailed information on the program, its resources, and its fund raising methods before agreeing to provide such support.

Even if you are only a minor contributor, you may want to think twice before allowing a charitable group to use your business's name. Some organizations have been known to use the names of contributors to pressure others to contribute.

If you decide to agree to the use of your company's name, ask for a signed agreement clearly specifying how, when, and where it may be used and confirming your right to review and approve advance copies of all print and audio/visual materials that contain references to your company. Soliciting organizations should honor requests for confidentiality and should not publicize the identity of donors without prior written permission. Organizations that violate this trust should be brought to the attention of local Better Business Bureaus and the Council of Better Business Bureaus' Philanthropic Advisory Service (See Appendix B).

Offers of Merchandise

When asked to buy merchandise, services, advertising space, or tickets to a fund raising event in support of a worthy cause, consider whether you would make the purchase if there were no charitable "pitch." If not, consider whether backing the event will provide the maximum benefit to those you want to help.

Be wary of approaches that ask you to commit your company to buying "four tickets again this year." Was there a "last year"? What is the nature of the event? Whom will the purchase help?

If you are not really interested in the offered item, service, or event but would like to help the organization, consider a direct contribution—the full amount of which would benefit the charity. Then send your check directly to the charity, not to the promotion office.

If you decide to make the purchase, remember that only part of the purchase price is tax deductible. Only the amount of money that *exceeds* what the Internal Revenue Service calls the "fair market value" of the item or service is considered a donation for tax purposes. For example, if you pay ten dollars for a box of candy that normally sells for eight dollars, only the two-dollar difference can be claimed as a charitable contribution (See page 44, "When Can You Deduct?").

Some Final Tips

In considering charitable contributions, keep the following guidelines in mind.

- Ask questions, and don't give until you are satisfied with the answers. Charities with nothing to hide will encourage your interest. Be wary of those reluctant to answer reasonable questions.

- Mail appeals should clearly identify the charity and describe its programs. Beware of appeals that bring tears to your eyes but tell you nothing about the charity or how its work addresses the problems depicted. Appeals should not be disguised as invoices. It is illegal to mail a bill or statement of account due that is in fact an appeal for funds, unless it bears a clear and noticeable disclaimer. See page 34 for guidelines on how to handle solicitations disguised as invoices.

- It is against the law to demand payment for unordered merchandise. If unordered items such as key rings, stamps, greeting cards, or pens are enclosed with an appeal letter, you are under no obligation to pay for or return the merchandise. See pages 26 to 27 for guidelines on handling cases involving unordered merchandise.

- Before buying candy, magazine subscriptions, cards, or tickets to a dinner or show to benefit a charity, ask what the charity's share will be. And keep in mind that only a portion of the amount paid for any such item is tax deductible.

- Don't be misled by a name that looks impressive or resembles the name of a well-known organization.

- Always make your contribution by check, and make the check out to the charity, not to the individual collecting the donation.

- Keep receipts and canceled checks so you can document your charitable giving at tax time. Although the value of your time as a volunteer is not deductible, out-of-pocket expenses that directly relate to your volunteer services, such as transportation costs, may be deductible. Again, keep records of such expenses.

- Check out local soliciting organizations with your local Better Business Bureau (See Appendix B). For information on national fund raising organizations, contact the Philanthropic Advisory Service of the Council of Better Business Bureaus (Appendix B).

- Call your local Better Business Bureau and local police department if a fund raiser uses high-pressure tactics, such as intimidation, threats, or repeated and harrassing phone calls or visits.

 IF YOU ARE VICTIMIZED

If you believe you have been the victim of a deceptive charity plea, you can file a complaint against the soliciting organization by contacting your local Better Business Bureau (See Appendix B), the Internal Revenue Service (Appendix A), or your state attorney general's office, listed under state government in most telephone directories. Complaints about national charities may be directed to the Philanthropic Advisory Service (Appendix B).

Many states have consumer protection agencies and special offices to regulate charities. See your telephone directory listings under state government.

CHAPTER 4

THE CASE OF

The Vanishing Broker

A midwestern farmer needs funds to upgrade his business by installing a new, highly mechanized irrigation system. Unfortunately, due to cash flow problems and unexpected personal expenses, he is in arrears with his mortgage and tractor loan payments. Scanning the business section of his Sunday newspaper, he spots a small ad offering loans on a "non-secured basis to credit-worthy individuals." He calls the listed phone number and makes an appointment.

At a suite in an airport hotel, the farmer meets a "loan broker" who listens to the details of his farm improvement plan and assures him that his enterprise is precisely the type for which a loan can be secured. The broker fills out several official-looking "loan application" forms, which the farmer signs. A check for $15,000 will be on its way, the broker assures the farmer, within ten working days. All that is needed is the "agreed-upon" check for $875 in "advance loan fees" plus another $125 to process the loan.

Loan Broker Frauds
and
"Advance Fee" Schemes

Although the farmer is startled to hear that he must pay $1,000 to get the loan, the broker assures him this is standard practice. They agree to meet the following day—time enough for the farmer to float a temporary loan from relatives. The broker arranges to pick up a cashier's check for $1,000 at the farm. Two weeks pass, and the farmer, anxious because he hasn't heard from the broker, pulls out his copy of the loan agreement and calls the listed phone number. The phone has been disconnected. Further inquiry reveals that the post office box listed as the broker's local address has been closed.

Monetary Matchmakers

Loan brokering is a legitimate business activity. But a growing number of businesspeople who have become discouraged by high interest rates and hard-to-find risk or investment capital are falling victim to swindlers operating loan broker schemes. The FBI estimates that each year American businesses are swindled out of millions of dollars by fraudulent loan brokers.

To examine how unscrupulous loan brokers practice their illegal schemes, we first must take a look at the way their legitimate counterparts operate.

Legitimate loan brokers generally are respected members of the business community who specialize in bringing together those in need of capital with those who have money to lend. The interest rate on these loans frequently is tied to the prime interest rate, the rate that banks charge their top-rated corporate borrowers. Depending on size and security, business and consumer loans may be several percentage points higher than the prime rate.

A loan broker may or may not require what is called an "advance fee" or deposit before providing any services. Even among legitimate brokers, advance fees are not uncommon, and they may not always be refundable, regardless of whether the loan is obtained. In addition, if the broker locates the loan money, the client usually pays a percentage of the total received at the time the loan becomes effective.

The fees a loan broker charges usually are high, but to the borrower, finding the money needed to save a business may be worth almost any price.

Sorry, Wrong Number

Over the past decade, many local Better Business Bureaus have conducted surveys of questionable loan activities in the advance fee loan business. Brokers were asked what kinds of services they offered; the amount, if any, of advance fee charged; the dollar volume of funds located for clients in a 12-month period; and the main source—advance fees or percentages of located funds—of their income. Bureaus also asked for customer and banking references. In many cases brokers refused to reply, and follow-up calls found some broker phones disconnected. You might well find it enlightening to contact your local Better Business Bureau before doing business with a loan broker.

Variations on the Scheme

Complaint files at local BBBs disclose a number of variations on advance fee loan schemes. In most fraudulent cases, a broker fee is paid, and the broker drops out of sight, goes "out of business," or points out that the fine print on the signed contracts makes no guarantee of funding.

When a business seeks a refund of the advance fee because the broker has failed to provide an agreed-upon number of lender referrals, the broker may provide the names of potential lenders who in reality have little or no interest in lending the money, or the broker may employ any of a variety of excuses to withhold the refund.

In some of the most brazen, yet successful, schemes, brokers offer to provide contacts with potential sources of investment capital. Then, advance fee in hand, these con artists fulfill their obligations (at least under the letter of the law) by mailing lists containing the names and addresses of local banks, savings and loan associations, and other financial institutions.

PROTECT YOUR BUSINESS

If your business is seeking a commercial loan through a broker, the answers to certain questions can help you to distinguish the legitimate operations from the schemes. Ask that the following information be provided to you in writing at least three days before any contract is signed and three days before you pay any broker fees.

1. The name and address of the broker.

2. The length of time the broker has been in business.

3. The total number of contracts the broker has signed in the preceding 12 months.

4. The number of successful contracts brokered in the preceding 12 months.

5. A complete description of services offered by the broker.

6. A full description of the broker's refund policy, including circumstances where you would not obtain a full refund even if no funding is received. (Some contracts provide that, if a loan is not obtained, the advance fee be refunded "after accounting for expenses incurred in preparing the application." But the fraudulent loan broker may manage to compute those expenses

so they just equal or slightly exceed the fee paid. If a contract contains such a clause, you should insist on a firm estimate of the nature of the expenses to be charged back and the anticipated total of those expenses.)

You should also insist on receiving a copy of the broker agreement.

Think Like a Banker

Even if, for one reason or another, your business is not seeking a loan through a bank, you may find it worthwhile to compare the approach a bank loan officer would take with that of the broker you are considering.

The bank loan officer will first scrutinize your business, its financial condition, and the purpose of the loan. The bank in all likelihood will not want to become involved in the operation of your business, but it will want to be assured that you have done your homework and are qualified to operate the business. The only way the lender can receive these assurances is to examine the answers to a number of questions.

For example, if you are buying a business, the loan officer will want to know how much it will cost per month to keep the doors open, how much business you must do each month to generate that amount, and whether the previous owners did that much business. The lender will be interested in your contingency plans for emergencies. Are you creating a cash reserve? Can you reduce expenses? You will probably be cross-examined about the accuracy of your projections and monthly cash flow analysis.

The point is that any legitimate loan broker or financial loan officer will want accurate, clear-cut answers to questions about your business. The primary concern of a representative of a legitimate loan organization will be to ascertain that the loan will be repaid promptly and that if it is defaulted on, some form of backup or collateral exists.

With this in mind, be cautious of:

- Loan brokers who pay little attention to potential risks.

- Brokers who attempt to discourage you from looking more closely at the lending institution by bringing in a lawyer or financial adviser.

- Brokers who continually divert your inquiries by extolling your business prospects.

- A long list of references or satisfied customers who, for one reason or another, cannot be contacted and may not exist. Also be wary of references who immediately give a good report, without taking the time to check their records. They could be accomplices paid to sit by the telephone and wait for calls like yours.

- Brokers who claim no form of collateral is needed beyond your good intentions.

- Brokers who list their offices as post office boxes or impressive-sounding, possibly nonexistent, addresses.

- Brokers who continually arrange meetings at hotels, airports, or restaurants, and who have no permanent base of operations that can be conveniently visited.

- Brokers who need "up front" money to help operate their businesses. You should in any case place advance money in an escrow account.

Because they are regulated industries, banks and savings and loan institutions are more strict in their requirements and less likely to handle "problem loans" than typical loan brokers. Be careful, though, because alternative lenders can be much tougher to deal with if you cannot repay the loan as agreed.

The SBA Alternative

If you have been turned down for a loan from a bank, you may be entitled to apply for assistance from the federal government's Small Business Administration (SBA). Your bank loan officer can help you apply for SBA assistance, and if you are accepted, the SBA will guarantee your loan from the bank.

The SBA is primarily interested in providing loan assurances to small businesses that:

- Are located in areas where there is a high percentage of unemployment

- Are owned by low-income proprietors

- Have been damaged by hurricanes, earthquakes, or other natural disasters

- Have been displaced by various actions of the federal government

---

Shop Around

Even if your regular bank is not the selected source of funding, your banker usually will be willing to talk with you about your plans. His or her advice and referrals could be very useful.

If your banker cannot help you and you find that your business does not qualify for an SBA guarantee, you can shop around for other potential sources of funds by contacting organizations listed in the phone book under loans or financial services.

Your approach to obtaining a commercial loan should not be much different from shopping for the best deal on a house, appliance, or other major purchase. Speak with a wide variety of people, make certain all your questions are answered satisfactorily, and don't hesitate to seek outside professional advice.

The reputation that your potential loan broker has in the community can provide a good indication of his business conduct. Ask the opinions of business colleagues who have had similar needs, and don't be reluctant to ask the lender for a list of references and to check those references.

Be certain that you understand everything involved with the loan before you sign any documents. If in doubt, consult an attorney, accountant, or financial adviser.

Before you enter into an arrangement with a loan broker, consider these questions.

☐ **Have you explored all the alternatives** to an "advance fee" loan broker?

☐ **Is the broker using sources** available to you directly?

☐ **Is a distant lender more likely** to assist you through a loan broker than traditional sources close to home—particularly if you already have been turned down by those local sources?

 IF YOU ARE VICTIMIZED

If you believe you have been the victim of an advance fee loan scam, file both verbal and written complaints with the local branch of the FBI, listed in your telephone directory, and your local Better Business Bureau (See Appendix B). If any of the elements of the scheme, such as contracts or agreements, were sent through the U.S. mail, also contact your local U.S. Postal Service office and the Chief Postal Inspector, U.S. Postal Service (Appendix A). It is important that you assemble and save all the documents involved in the transaction, along with names, addresses, telephone numbers, and other pertinent information.

The BBB and the FBI or Postal Service can help you determine whether you indeed have been the victim of an illegal operation. If such is the case, contact your attorney for advice and assistance in pursuing your case.

CHAPTER 5

THE CASE OF

The Menacing Merchants

The new owners of a men's clothing store announce intentions of widening their selection and eventually expanding into a chain of clothing and accessories stores. Accomplishing their ambitious plans will require a large amount of capital, and so, they explain to suppliers, they must depart from the previous owner's policy of paying for all purchases within 30 days. With suppliers' cooperation, the expansion plans should quickly lead to bigger orders and increased profits for all.

The new owners also convince local bankers to provide secondary mortgage funds to augment their "working capital."

As new clothing and accessories orders begin to pour in, the owners place a few of each item on store shelves and secretly ship the remainder to a warehouse several hundred miles away. While some of the "working capital" is used to spruce up the store, most is quietly routed out of town.

Bankruptcy Fraud

With credit extended to the hilt, the owners spring the trap. Their store ostensibly is broken into and stripped of its merchandise. The police are summoned, an investigation ensues, several leads are followed, but the case eventually dead-ends. The store owners, it is disclosed, had no business insurance; they have no alternative but to file for bankruptcy.

Creditors wrangle over the few remaining worthwhile assets, and most are left with substantial losses. The owners assist in the final stages of bankruptcy, and several months later, slip out of town—to claim their secreted funds and quietly arrange for the sale of the stored merchandise.

The Changing Face of Crime

In its simplest form, bankruptcy fraud involves the purchase of merchandise on credit, the surreptitious sale of the merchandise, concealment of the proceeds, and subsequent filing for bankruptcy.

The U.S. Department of Justice estimates that bankruptcy fraud costs American businesses and consumers well in excess of $100 million a year. Hardest hit are small businesses that unknowingly sell goods on credit to swindlers.

Historically, organized crime and individual con artists have carried out the majority of these schemes. Recently, however, a strong trend has developed in which formerly honest businesspersons, hoping to save something for themselves from the crumbling structure of their failing businesses, turn to fraud. These white-collar criminals have been known to operate from the highest levels of the corporate world, so no one today is above the scrutiny of law enforcement officials.

Recent changes in the federal bankruptcy laws, argue some business and law enforcement officials, have created an environment that encourages bankruptcy fraud to flourish. When a business files for bankruptcy, the court seizes its property and sells whatever the law permits it to sell, with the proceeds divided among the creditors. With some exceptions, the court erases the business's prior debts. Under a 1979 change in the federal bankruptcy code, those filing for bankruptcy can retain more of their possessions than ever before. As a result, some have found it more financially attractive to opt for bankruptcy than to work their way out of a financial crisis. And some businesspersons intending to file for bankruptcy take advantage of today's more lenient bankruptcy codes to actually improve their personal financial position.

A Variety of Schemes

The many ingenious variations on bankruptcy fraud include:

☐ **The creation of a bogus company.** A company is formed by simply depositing a moderate amount of money in a bank account to establish credit. Misleading balance sheets and income statements are prepared for the inspection of potential victims.

☐ **Company takeovers.** A business with financial problems, usually one that is well known in the community, is purchased with a minimal downpayment. While the new owners might begin their operation by paying cash for small orders, the volume of orders quickly grows and a line of credit is established. The goods are sold at bargain prices or secretly moved to another location, and the business folds—thanks to "poor business practices," an overnight "robbery," fire damage, or some other "unexpected catastrophe."

☐ **Failed business.** The long-time owner of a legitimate firm sees bankruptcy as the best way out of a failing business. Buying, spending, and credit practices may be orchestrated to result in a profitable bankruptcy.

☐ **Bust-outs.** In this variation of the above three schemes, the proprietors do not file for bankruptcy—they leave town. While not literally a form of bankruptcy, a bust-out includes many of the elements of bankruptcy fraud.

  ## PROTECT YOUR BUSINESS

Be wary of the following tell-tale signs of bankruptcy fraud.

- A sudden change in a business's management, particularly a change occurring without public notice.

- A business that lists only a post office box as its contact point.

- A business that uses an answering service.

- A customer whose credit balance begins to climb dramatically.

- A new customer that suddenly begins to place many orders on credit, or one that switches from paying cash to strictly credit.

- A new customer whose credit references either cannot be contacted or give a good report immediately, without looking at records. The unreachable references may not exist; their overeager counterparts may be parties to the scheme.

- Rush orders, particularly those of substantial numbers, from a new customer or from a business that previously has not placed orders in any great quantity.

- A business with a prestigious-sounding name or a name that is strikingly similar to that of a well-established and well-financed company.

If in doubt, remember that your Better Business Bureau (See Appendix B) can provide you with information on the reliability of a local business. While much of the information in BBB reports deals with customer experiences with the subject, the BBB also can provide data on company principals, government actions, and prior bankruptcy proceedings.

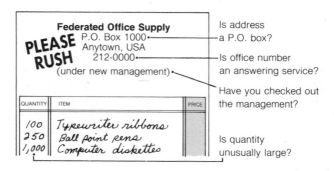

IF YOU ARE VICTIMIZED

Because many of the signs of an impending bankruptcy fraud are also commonplace among legitimate enterprises merely experiencing slow business periods, bankruptcy fraud usually goes undetected until it is too late.

If an occurrence of those warning signs described on pages 59 to 60 makes you believe that a bankruptcy fraud is imminent, curtail further transactions with the suspect business, stop deliveries of goods, prevent further credit allowances, and state clearly that payment is overdue and is expected without delay.

It is, of course, important that you not spread what could turn out to be false and damaging rumors. However, if you strongly suspect an element of foul play, contact the local offices of the FBI and the office of your local District Attorney, both of which should be listed in your telephone directory. Be prepared to provide details of your business arrangement with the suspect business and your reasons for suspecting fraud. A number of areas of the law could come into play in a bankruptcy fraud, including, among others, the illegal falsification of business records, the defrauding of secured creditors, fraud in insolvency, the public issuance of false financial statements, and the receipt of deposits in a failing financial institution.

CHAPTER 6

A CASE OF

Bitter Sweets

A worker dissatisfied with his salary and his 9 to 5 routine comes across a magazine ad offering an opportunity to enter the "rapidly expanding, lucrative vending machine business." If managed properly, the ad proclaims, this business can lead the investor to earn unlimited income "by working the hours you want to work." For an initial investment of $1,995, the applicant will receive complete ownership of his own equipment, plus the guarantee of a high-traffic location requiring minimal servicing. The ad's glowing testimonials from investors who have earned thousands of dollars in their spare time clinch the matter—the disgruntled worker, with high hopes for a profitable future, sends in a check for $1,995.

The vending machine that eventually arrives is a cheaply-made candy dispenser, complete with an introductory supply of off-brand

Business Opportunity
and
Investment Schemes

candy. Additional candy supplies are available only from the vending machine company. The "high-traffic" location turns out to be a nearby roadside reststop where several other vending machines offer similar products.

During his first six months of operation, the worker's average monthly profit is $25—or, considering transportation costs, supplies, and the time involved in servicing the machine, just over $2 for each hour worked.

When the vending machine breaks down, the owner finds that its warranty has expired and that repairs will cost $150. He attempts to repair the machine himself, and, failing that, throws it in his basement, where it will become a permanent, unpleasant reminder of his bad investment.

Business Opportunities Abound

The opportunity to "be your own boss," "work your own hours," and earn "unlimited amounts of money" attracts thousands of Americans each year. And, of course, many business opportunity offers are both legitimate and profitable. According to a U.S. Department of Commerce estimate, in 1984 independent salespeople generated retail sales of $8.5 billion, and retail franchises, the most popular form of business opportunity, accounted for about $401.2 billion, or 32 percent of all retail sales. Unfortunately, as these opportunities expand, a growing number of con artists move in, with the intent of making it difficult for those wishing to enter the field to distinguish the bona fide opportunities from the schemes.

The Federal Trade Commission (FTC), which regulates some of the activities of independent businesses, notes that while it is impossible to estimate the number of people defrauded by business opportunity schemes, annual losses may run into the billions of dollars. One reason statistics are hard to come by is that the variety of schemes seems virtually limitless. Among the most common are schemes practiced in the areas of:

- Franchising
- Vending machines
- Mail-order businesses
- Multi-level marketing
- Securities and commodity futures investment
- Land development
- Invention marketing
- Work-at-home enterprises

Inside the Schemes

Franchising

In the past 20 years, franchising has become one of the most popular ways for Americans to start their own businesses. Through franchising, a company achieves rapid and effective distribution of its products or services by sharing, through contractual agreement, its economic means and the possibility for profits with independent businesspeople. The franchisor may provide only a trademark and method of doing business, or a product or entire line of products.

THE NUMBER OF FRANCHISED COMPANIES HAS FLUCTUATED
(in thousands)

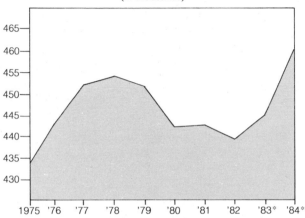

WHILE SALES OF GOODS AND SERVICES HAVE RISEN STEADILY
(in millions of dollars)

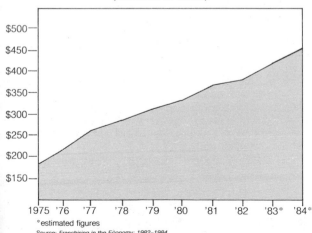

*estimated figures

Source: *Franchising in the Economy: 1982–1984*
U.S. Department of Commerce

While the majority of franchisors are legitimate, a growing number operate under false pretenses. In these cases, the victim may be subjected to a fast-paced, high-pressure sales pitch—complete with fictitious sales projections, testimonials, and slick promotional brochures—in which he is urged to act immediately to take advantage of a "ground floor" opportunity. After a sale has been completed and money collected, any of a number of possible scenarios may ensue.

Act II: After the Sale

☐ The sales representative—and the company represented—disappear with the investment.

☐ The franchisor goes out of business.

☐ Products or services turn out to be inferior, overpriced, or unmarketable.

☐ The franchise location is untrafficked.

☐ The specialized training promised by the franchisor is insufficient or nonexistent.

☐ Field support from the franchisor is inadequate.

☐ Advertising or promotions promised by the franchisor are inadequate or nonexistent.

☐ Whatever the reason, the investor duped into purchasing a business franchise under false pretenses sees plans for success fall to pieces.

Vending machines (including video games)

Like franchising frauds, vending machine frauds are aimed at investors hoping to tap a time-tested, nationally recognized consumer market. The victim of this type of scheme usually relies on the vending company to select the product, equipment, and optimal location. Often, the outcome is similar to the scams listed under "Act II" above. Additional factors in the failure of fraudulently sold businesses include:

- Machines placed in arcades or other locations where numerous other machines offer similar or better products

- Machines that do not work properly

- Vending supplies that cannot be sold at a reasonable profit

- Machines that require servicing and refilling far more time-consuming than anticipated

Mail-order businesses

In 1983, according to the Direct Marketing Association, mail-order catalogs, newspaper and magazine advertisements, and direct-mail solicitations accounted for U.S. consumer purchases of $63.4 billion—nearly double total purchases of only five years earlier. Given these rapidly rising statistics, it is not surprising that many mail-order entrepreneurs have become wealthy by offering to help others tap into this vast and lucrative marketplace. Unfortunately, some of these seemingly honest business brokers are actually in the business of conning luckless individuals out of hard-earned start-up capital, with

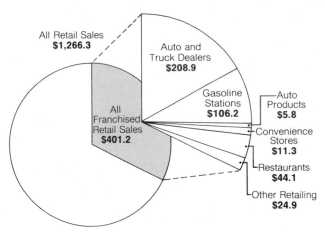

**FRANCHISING TO ENCOMPASS
32% OF RETAIL SALES IN '84**

(in billions of dollars)

All Retail Sales
$1,266.3

Auto and
Truck Dealers
$208.9

Gasoline
Stations
$106.2

Auto
Products
$5.8

All
Franchised
Retail Sales
$401.2

Convenience
Stores
$11.3

Restaurants
$44.1

Other Retailing
$24.9

Source: *Franchising in the Economy 1982–1984*
U.S. Department of Commerce

the consequent costs of time and effort wasted in working toward an unattainable goal.

Mail-order business opportunities commonly are offered through advertisements in newspapers, magazines, and business journals. The ads may promise would-be entrepreneurs the chance to supplement their income by selling products through the mail. Huge returns, with virtually no expense or labor, are promised. But in reality, the products offered by the promoter, either directly or through unnamed suppliers, are shoddy, stale, and of dubious sales appeal. Of equally dubious value are the instructions, catalogs, mailing lists, and advice some promoters provide.

Multi-level marketing

A legitimate form of retailing, multi-level marketing is a system in which independent businesspeople, often known as distributors, sell the products or services of a multi-level marketing company to small businesses or consumers. Most sales are made in customers' homes, and distributors set their own hours, with earning levels dependent upon the extent of their efforts and sales ability.

Most multi-level marketing companies encourage distributors to build and manage their own sales forces by recruiting, training, supplying, and motivating others to sell the products or services. Distributors who recruit other distributors are rewarded with a percentage based on the sales of their entire sales force.

Legitimate multi-level marketing companies stress that there is no easy path to riches—that success can come only through consistent dedication and hard work.

Pyramid schemes, also known as "chain letter" schemes, are illegal variations of the multi-level marketing system. The emphasis in a pyramid scheme is on the quick profits to be earned by recruiting others, who in turn will recruit others, and so on—with each new recruit paying a specified sum which goes to those higher up in the chain. Although promotional literature or sales pitches may present this as a business opportunity, the merchandise or service to be sold is largely ignored, and, in fact, there may be little potential for actually making sales.

In some pyramid schemes, there *is* no product or service, or the product exists only in token form to show others that the individual is a member of the "sales team." These members are then paid commissions or bonuses for recruiting other investors, who also receive token products. Scant mention is made of the fact that the ever-increasing number of participants, all attempting to recoup their investments by recruiting from the ever-decreasing ranks of potential investors in a given area, will quickly result in market saturation.

Millions of dollars are lost each year in pyramid schemes, with the hardest-hit victims those people with little knowledge of business and limited means who can least afford to lose their "investments."

Pyramids: Pointless Pursuit

Consider the results if one person recruited six distributors, each of whom in turn recruited six others, and carry the process through nine steps as follows:

	1
1	6
2	36
3	216
4	1,296
5	7,776
6	46,656
7	279,936
8	1,679,616
9	10,077,696

At more than ten million people for every nine steps in the distribution program, the distributors soon would be recruiting one another. In order for everyone to profit in a pyramid scheme, there would have to be a never-ending supply of potential (and willing) participants. Obviously, there isn't. When the supply runs out, the pyramid collapses and most participants lose their investment.

Securities and commodity futures investment

As its name implies, securities investment requires that an investor place trust in the stability and future growth of a business or organization. In the case of a stock purchase, the investor hopes that a company's profitability and inherent value will grow, thereby increasing the value of its stock and the amount of dividend paid. In the case of bond investment, an individual lends money to a business at an agreed-upon interest rate plus the eventual maturity, or payback, of the loan. Other forms of security transactions include investment contracts and limited partnerships.

The investor in commodity futures agrees to buy or sell a pre-arranged amount of a commodity, such as precious metals, livestock, or government issuances, at a future date and at an agreed-upon price.

Most criminal activities in this area involve the sale of fraudulently represented properties. Examples include the sale of counterfeit or stolen securities, schemes that rely on the deceitful practices of traders or employees "inside" stock or bond clearinghouses, and international schemes involving sales of securities in nonexistent companies.

The swindlers generally are smooth-talking, persuasive individuals who try to overwhelm their targets. Telephone solicitors contact hundreds of prospects a day in search of the few who seem receptive; then the real "professional" comes on the line and attempts to close the sale. A messenger may be dispatched to pick up money immediately, before the victim has a chance to investigate or reconsider the offer.

Fraudulent commodity sales operations may use glossy brochures touting trading "successes." They may adopt a legitimate-sounding name and impressive mailing address—which in reality may be nothing more than a mail-drop or rented back office. Most of these questionable operations are not registered with any regulatory agency, even though, in most instances, registration with a regulatory body such as the Commodity Futures Trading Commission or the National Futures Association is mandatory for firms that deal with customers in commodity futures or options transactions.

Land development

Many business owners, investors, and consumers believe that land is always a good investment. Land fraud artists capitalize on that belief with schemes to sell or lease properties that have little or no tangible value.

Consumers are most frequently targeted by schemes to sell property ostensibly located in resort areas or urban developments which in reality is undesirable or unsuitable for reasonable use. Businesses may be duped into investing in inner-city business districts which turn out to be ramshackle buildings, or into leasing space in nonexistent, poorly situated, improperly financed, or inadequately insured business office buildings, co-ops, or condominiums.

Land fraud con artists usually employ high-pressure sales tactics. Their printed literature, usually sent through the mail, and their verbal sales pitches, often delivered by phone, may contain glittering generalities about the benefits of owning property in the bustling inner city or land in sunny resort locales. More specific, informative details are much more difficult to come by.

Invention marketing

Once you've invented the better mousetrap, how do you get it to market? Many legitimate invention marketing firms are in the business of helping investors with that problem; other fraudulent firms concentrate on collecting their victims' money while doing little or nothing to move their inventions to market.

Fraudulent firms may advertise in the same scientific and business journals, magazines, and news publications as their legitimate counterparts. The illegal operations may charge various "up front" fees for nonexistent services. They may promise to research the uniqueness of an invention, survey its marketability, obtain a patent, and produce and market the product. Con artists have been known to swindle inventors out of thousands of dollars by claiming they are developing a prototype or arranging for the mass production of an invention. But what these firms do best is swindle their unsuspecting victims by preying on vanity, emotions, hopes, and inexperience.

Work-at-home enterprises

Computers, products made at home, and services that can be offered from an office at home are creating new opportunities for individuals hoping to go into business for themselves by working from their homes. Yet the increasing interest in these "cottage industries" has its negative side. Today, a growing number of Americans are falling victim to work-at-home schemes. Federal law enforcement agencies explain that total losses by these victims are almost impossible to estimate. Most losses are under $100 and are never reported to authorities because victims wish to avoid the embarrassment or bother involved in filing a complaint.

Victims of work-at-home schemes usually are "hooked" through newspaper advertisements. A typical ad might offer to show the respondent how to "earn $100 a week by addressing envelopes in your spare time at home." Unsuspecting victims who mail their $19.95 for details are sent instructions on how to write and place similar ads in their own local newspapers.

Other more complex, costlier schemes might offer to set up the respondent in a full-fledged business enterprise. If you were to respond, you might be trained to produce, for example, a certain mechanical or electronic device which supposedly is part of a larger mechanism to be assembled by the mail-order company. The company guarantees it will purchase your products, and after investing several thousand dollars in training, equipment, and supplies, you begin turning out the devices and shipping them to the company. The devices are returned with a letter explaining that their quality is inferior and below standards. The small print in your signed contract explains that the mail-order firm has the option of rejecting products it considers unacceptable—and what it considers acceptable turns out to be beyond your reach.

 PROTECT YOURSELF

By the time you realize you have been the victim of a business opportunity fraud, it usually is too late. You have invested your money and the con artists most likely have closed up operations and moved on. Even if you are fortunate enough to catch the swindlers in the act, prosecution may prove difficult or impossible. And if you are able to prosecute and win your case, there is no guarantee you will recover any of the money you invested.

Therefore, precaution is your best line of defense.

1. **Find out as much as possible about the reliability of the firm offering the business opportunity.**

   ☐ Ask for financial statements for the past three years and verify that they have been audited by a reputable firm. Financial statements should include full details on operating revenues and source of revenues, as well as a profit and loss statement.

   ☐ Ask for evidence or research to support claims of growth potential and profitability, and have an accountant look it over.

   ☐ Ask for and check business, bank, and client references. Be wary if references seem to respond too quickly and eagerly; they may be accomplices waiting for such calls.

   ☐ Find out how long the firm has been in business, and ask for information on its litigation record. Look for lawsuits, bankruptcy proceedings, and charges of embezzlement, fraud, and unfair or deceptive practices.

☐ If the business opportunity involves door-to-door sales, find out if the firm is a member of the Direct Selling Association (See Appendix A).

☐ Remember that firms offering legitimate business opportunities are interested in answering your questions fully. If a firm cannot or will not answer key questions, you would be wise to avoid further involvement.

2. **Before you enter into a business arrangement, make certain you fully understand the responsibilities of all parties.** Have your attorney or accountant go over the details of the agreement.

In Securities and Commodity Futures

If you have questions about securities dealings, contact the U.S. Securities and Exchange Commission's (SEC) Office of Consumer Affairs or your regional SEC office (See Appendix A). You also may contact your state's securities administrator, listed in your telephone directory.

In questions involving possible commodity futures fraud, contact the Commodity Futures Trading Commission (CFTC) and your regional CFTC office (See Appendix A). You also may contact the National Futures Association (Appendix A), a self-regulatory organization to which membership is mandatory for any firm involved in commodity sales.

Also watch out for these warning signs of fraudulent investment activity.

- Unsolicited, high-pressure phone calls

- Claims of inside information

- "You must act at once!" warnings

- Forecasts of large, quick profits

- Claims of virtually no risk

- Contracts with names such as "deferred delivery," "fixed maturity," or "cash forward," which are not traded through regulated commodities exchanges. These contracts may be legal, but unlike those traded through regulated exchanges they do not carry many customer protection features.

73

In Franchising and Sales Opportunities

Be aware of the fact that the FTC requires franchisors to provide certain information at the earlier of either the first personal meeting to discuss a franchise purchase with the potential investor or no later than ten business days before the investor signs a franchise or related agreement or pays any money in connection with the purchase. This information includes: identifying information about the franchisor; background information on the business and its officers; and substantial details on how the franchise arrangement is to work and what restrictions, such as geographical boundaries to territories or conditions on the right to sell or transfer ownership, are to be placed on either party.

In the case of business opportunities that appear to guarantee "territorial rights," insist on a written explanation of the restrictions to be imposed upon you or upon potential competitors who also buy into the business.

In Invention Marketing

The FTC recommends that inventors shop for a marketing firm just as they would any major service provider. Ask for and contact references, including organizations and institutions with which the firm has dealt and other inventors who have been successfully marketed. Ask for a written curriculum vitae detailing academic and career achievements of each of the principals. Insist on a written explanation of fees and services.

The U.S. Patent Office points out that inventors can do some of the initial legwork themselves. A public patent search facility is located at 2021 Jefferson Davis Highway, Arlington, Virginia. The Patent Office, which issues some 50,000 patents annually, provides this facility so that individuals can determine whether patents have been issued for products or services similiar to their inventions. The Patent Office also publishes a booklet, "General Information Concerning Patents,"* containing a step-by-step guide to the patent process. In addition, you can contact the Commissioner of Patents and Trademarks, Washington, D.C. 20231, for a list of registered patent attorneys in your geographical area.

---

*Booklet is available for $1.75 per copy from the Superintendent of Documents, Government Printing Office, Washington, D.C. 20402.

In General

For general information about possibly fraudulent business practices in your area, contact your state's attorney general's office, listed under state government in most telephone directories.

3. **The actions and qualifications of sales agents may provide indications of the reliability of the firms they represent.**

   ☐ Be wary of sales agents who emphasize the profitability of recruiting others into the business, rather than making sales and providing exceptional service.

   ☐ Be wary of sales agents who offer you "free" merchandise as an inducement to buy.

   ☐ Check the qualifications of sales agents or dealers. Often the easiest way to do this is by contacting the associations that license agents in their area of specialty. For example, agents selling land or property must possess a real estate license issued by the state's real estate commission. That commission can tell you whether the agent is certified and has obtained the required training. Securities brokers and their firms must be registered with the SEC (See Appendix A), which can provide similar information.

4. **Be on the alert for the following signs of potentially fraudulent activity.**

   ☐ Be wary of business opportunities that promise quick or unusually high returns on "once-in-a-lifetime" investments. Ask yourself what might be behind such "rare" and generous offers.

   ☐ Be skeptical of "private sales" or offerings, particularly those in which substantial discounts are offered on so-called list prices.

   ☐ Don't be taken in by impressive-sounding company names or addresses.

   ☐ Be particularly cautious about doing business with firms located outside the U.S. It may become difficult or even impossible to trace and recover your money.

☐ Look closely at the quality of printed documents. Deeds, securities, guarantees, or other supposedly official documents may be counterfeits, and an unprofessional printing job could be the tip-off.

☐ Don't be fooled by initial easily obtained returns on your investment. A smooth con artist may use your investment to pay these returns, in order to entice you to invest even more heavily.

5. **Investigate before you invest.**

☐ Before buying or investing in an enterprise, product, or property, check with others in similar businesses to see if the price quoted is reasonable.

☐ Before buying into a sales or mail-order business, look carefully at the quality of the product or service, its potential market, your profit margin, and the reliability and background of the mail-order company.

☐ Before doing business with a firm, contact your local Better Business Bureau (See Appendix B) for a reliability report.

 IF YOU ARE VICTIMIZED

Business opportunity schemes are often carefully constructed to conform to the letter of the law. Or they may operate in a gray area of the law where rulings generally fall in their favor. Whatever the case, if you believe you have been the victim of a business opportunity scheme:

1. Contact your local police department.

2. Stop payment on checks in transit.

3. Contact the state or federal agencies that oversee activities in your area of concern and provide them with full details, in writing, of the fraud. For example, if victimized by a commodity futures fraud, you would send complete details to the CFTC, your regional CFTC office, and the National Futures Association. Addresses and phone numbers for these and other organizations and agencies can be found in Appendix A.

4. Call your local Better Business Bureau (see Appendix B), and send the Bureau copies of the material going to the federal or state agency.

While it is often difficult, if not impossible, to recoup losses suffered in a fraudulent business opportunity scheme, your efforts in contacting and informing the appropriate authorities may help to prevent others from being victimized.

SECTION II

EXTERNAL
CRIME

CHAPTER 7

THE CASE OF

The Buyer's Blues

The buyer for a major chain of discount department stores knows that customers would snap up a hot-selling new line of blue jeans. The jeans, distributed under a well-known designer label, feature large gold-tone zippers on the pockets and sides of the legs, and a sprightly devil patch on the back pocket. The problem is that the line's designer will only market her creations through certain selected retailers, and this discounter is not a part of that select list.

But the buyer has other sources—distributors who often can locate and purchase hard-to-find products. Working through such a middleman, the buyer is able to purchase a good quantity of the exclusive item at a good price. Soon, in stores all around the country, customers find the discounter's racks filled with the popular designer jeans, selling at a price that is several dollars lower than that offered in most other area stores. Sales are brisk, and management and customers alike are pleased.

Product Counterfeiting

. . . Until the returns begin to come in. Customers begin bringing back their purchases for refunds, and their complaints are monotonously similar. After only one or two wearings, the jeans' stylish zippers loosen and fall off. The discounter is forced to refund so many of the defective garments that it finally yanks the product off store shelves. The distributor is contacted and proves uncommunicative and uncooperative. Appeals are made to the manufacturer, which sends a representative to examine the jeans. The examination confirms the manufacturer's suspicions; the blue jeans are counterfeits—very good counterfeits at first glance, with style and stitching copied to the last detail, but a closer examination reveals that the materials and workmanship are shoddy. And the final tip-off is the back pocket patch. On the counterfeit jeans, the details on the devil's face and slippers are less defined. And he is carrying his pitchfork in the wrong hand.

An "Epidemic" of Frauds

According to the International Anticounterfeiting Coalition (IACC), a nonprofit organization consisting of large and small U.S. and foreign companies, firms, trade associations, and government agencies, the problem of commercial counterfeiting has reached "epidemic proportions." The federal government's International Trade Commission (ITC) estimates annual losses to U.S. businesses due to foreign counterfeiting and copyright and patent infringements at $6 billion to $8 billion. Many concerned businesspeople and lawmakers say the figure actually may be much higher—in 1983, perhaps as high as $18 billion, according to the U.S. Customs Service.

Foreign counterfeiting was responsible for the loss of more than 130,000 U.S. jobs in 1982, says the ITC. Again, others suspect a much higher degree of damage. According to a 1983 Automotive Parts and Accessories Association estimate, in the automotive products industry alone, 300,000 jobs a year are lost due to counterfeiting.

Whatever the figures, product counterfeiting clearly is a lucrative international business growing at an alarming rate, with devastating consequences for corporations and consumers in the U.S. and abroad.

From High Fashion to High Tech

Commercial counterfeiting began on a small scale with blue jeans, Swiss watches, and fashion accessories. Today, a wide range of products are involved, including cosmetics, sporting goods, records and tapes, drugs and medical equipment, aircraft parts, and Army missile systems parts. Counterfeits have even been found among parts to be used in a test of the U.S. space shuttle.

The dangers go beyond the real economic hazards of lost domestic jobs and tax dollars. When a manufacturer's product is copied and mass-produced, the victimized company loses sales and profits. When a counterfeit product of inferior quality gives the consumer problems, the company suffers damage to perhaps its most priceless commodity—its reputation. And when the counterfeit is a shoddy copy of a heart pump, an automobile brake shoe, or a commercial helicopter or airliner part, health and safety are threatened.

Counterfeits and knock-offs are related sides of the same bad coin. Counterfeits are exact copies of a product, designed to have as great a similarity to the real thing— down to brand name and logotype—as the counterfeiter's art can achieve. Knock-offs are near-copies packaged to look just like the original, often including logo and emblems, but with a slight difference in the brand name or with the addition of the word "replaces" in extremely small type before the forged logo. The bogus goods may be imported as complete counterfeits, or labels, logos, and emblems may be applied after the items have entered the country.

According to the ITC, most production of counterfeits and knock-offs takes place in the Far East, in countries including Taiwan, Hong Kong, Indonesia, Singapore, South Korea, and the Philippines. Other sources are Latin America (particularly Brazil, Colombia, and Mexico), Europe, the Middle East, the Peoples Republic of China, and Africa (primarily Nigeria). Counterfeit goods enter the U.S. from more than 40 nations, but America is not the only country feeling the effects of this rising crime wave. France's Union des Fabricants has estimated annual losses to its members at $290 million, and Swiss watch manufacturers maintain that counterfeiters sell about ten million bogus Swiss watches per year, with illegal revenues of perhaps $500 million.

Even more than the industrialized nations, Third World countries are experiencing a flood of fakes. Counterfeits of American or European-made products are easily distributed in Third World countries where customers who cannot read the labels identify the popular foreign items by the appearance of the packages.

In many ways, a company's success contributes to its vulnerability to the counterfeiting of its designs, trademarks, and copyrights. The counterfeiter's business is built on popular products with distinctive packaging and international recognition. Cashing in on the investment the manufacturer has made in research and development and in creating a demand in a particular market, the counterfeiter is able to mass-produce a copy at a cost far below that required to produce the real thing. Contributing to low costs are the illicit business's freedom from taxes, research and development expenses, advertising and promotional costs, and social security payments, plus cheap labor, inferior materials, and shoddy construction.

While most copies are of inferior quality, in some cases the quality of a fake can be so good that even experts may have difficulty telling the difference. One area where counterfeiting is particularly hard to identify and prevent is in pirated computer software. Pirates can easily and inexpensively make copies of software that others have spent months or even years developing. Beyond the devastating losses in sales and profits, U.S. computermakers are concerned that the almost instantaneous theft and mass distribution of their creations could chip away at this country's position as the world's leader in technology.

Cracking Down

As long as there are cost-conscious consumers looking for brand names and distinctive designs at bargain prices—and unscrupulous companies and individuals ready to exploit that market—there will be counterfeiting. U.S. businesses and lawmakers hope only that efforts at prevention, detection, and retribution will increase the risks and lower the profits of the miscreants.

Many U.S. firms spend upwards of one million dollars annually to finance the war on counterfeiting. The most effective weapons in their arsenal include lawsuits against illicit overseas and domestic operations, detectives who gather and pass on leads, new anticounterfeiting technology, and consumer education.

Fighting counterfeiting through the different legal systems of foreign countries takes a significant investment of time and money. While there has been some cooperation by a few of the developing nations considered primary sources of bogus goods, legislation and enforcement remain lax. Still, U.S. firms that have concertedly pursued suits against offenders in foreign countries have in some cases achieved a measure of success in stymieing the offenders. Private investigation firms have often played a vital role in providing the information needed to bring suit. Private detectives employed by U.S. and foreign firms monitor suspect factories and retail outfits and pass on leads that help the firms track down, close down, and sometimes prosecute the perpetrators.

New electronic, optical, and computer-designed technology also helps make the counterfeiter's job more difficult. Credit card companies are trying new laser technology that is expensive but effective. (See Chapter 10, Credit Card Fraud.) Recording companies are considering the use of hard-to-imitate high-tech labels that contain thousands of microscopic lenses over a distinctive pattern or logo. Other antifraud measures coming into use include "fingerprinted" labels, each printed with its own computer-generated code number. The authenticity of a label can be verified only by the system that generated its code number, thus enabling the manufacturer to easily identify counterfeits and the stores where they're being sold. Yet even with all these state-of-the-art devices, says the IACC, manufacturers are fighting an almost hopeless battle. As soon as a new technology is unveiled, counterfeiters begin to explore ways to imitate it—and most often, they succeed.

Manufacturers are by no means alone in the battlefield. In 1983, the federal government, through the U.S. Customs Service, began a major drive to combat all types of fraudulent import practices, with a particular emphasis on the importing of counterfeit goods. By mid-

1984, more than 40 special Customs Service fraud investigation teams were inspecting goods coming into major airports and seaports across the country. Some manufacturers have cooperated with Customs officials by providing detailed product descriptions, and the IACC has conducted seminars for Customs officials at ports throughout the United States, but, say investigators, more information is needed on many more products. Furthermore, companies hoping to keep illegal copies of their products out of this country must record their registered trademarks and copyrights with the Customs Service. Without such recordals, even if investigators spot a shipment of fakes, they by law are not permitted to seize the bogus goods.

 PROTECT YOUR BUSINESS

We have already discussed some of the steps being taken by manufacturers to foil counterfeiters. The following measures can help you protect your business.

1. **Register all trademarks** with the U.S. Patent and Trademark Office and record them with the U.S. Customs Service and with foreign customs.

2. **Register all copyrights** with the U.S. Copyright Office and record them with the U.S. Customs Service and with foreign customs.

3. **Alert your sales force,** distributors, and manufacturers to the counterfeiting problem, and instruct them to look for counterfeits at retail establishments and trade shows.

4. **Educate consumers** to the counterfeiting problem and how to distinguish the fakes. Investigate all consumer complaints about the inauthenticity of products.

5. **Hire private investigators** to monitor retail establishments for counterfeits and to find their sources.

6. **Encourage federal and state law enforcement and consumer agencies** to aggressively pursue cases of product counterfeiting.

7. **Set up a permanent department** to investigate and prosecute counterfeiting cases.

For further advice and information, you might want to contact the IACC (See Appendix A), which has set up an exchange program to help companies share information on investigators, counsel, litigation, detection techniques, and other key elements of an effective anticounterfeiting program. The IACC also has instituted a product authentification service for consumers, to assist in the identification of counterfeit products.

The best approach retailers can take to avoid becoming a party to the distribution of bogus goods is founded on common sense. Deal with reputable distributors only, and be wary when a distributor says it will be easy delivering what you know is a hard-to-find product. If a deal seems too good to be true, it probably is.

 # IF YOU ARE VICTIMIZED

The most effective response to the counterfeiting of your company's designs, trademarks, and copyrights is multi-faceted. Your actions should involve tracking down the source of the bogus goods, pushing for the enforcement of existing antifraud laws, and, through the measures discussed earlier, moving to prevent further counterfeiting.

Many manufacturers hire trademark and patent attorneys who use private detectives to locate the source of counterfeit products. Evidence then can be presented to a judge, who may order the suspect goods seized. Consult your attorney in any case involving the investigation and prosecution of counterfeiting activities.

Until recently, even if a counterfeiter could be brought to justice, penalties were insufficient to deter counterfeiting in the U.S. However, legislation was passed by Congress in 1984 that imposes strict criminal and financial penalties and provides strengthened civil remedies. A measure also was passed by Congress in 1984 that puts pressure on foreign governments to act against counterfeiting within their borders or risk losing significant trade benefits.

The IACC information exchange program can provide current data on legislation, enforcement, and on techniques for combatting known or suspected counterfeits.

CHAPTER 8

THE CASE OF

The Sticky Tickets

After a large weekend sale, the staff of a department store completes an inventory of remaining merchandise. A review of sales receipts and inventory sheets reveals that a large number of sale items that supposedly were sold remain on display, while similar nonsale items have disappeared.

After reviewing the situation with sales clerks and cashiers, the manager concludes that a number of dishonest customers must have

Crimes Practiced
on Cashiers

---

peeled the price tags off sale items and transferred them to similar, but more expensive, nonsale items.

Cashiers, accustomed to looking at price tags rather than merchandise, rang up the more expensive items at the sale prices. As a result, inventory write-offs for this one major sale were more than $100,000.

Cashier Rip-offs: A Retailer's Nightmare

Price tag switching is just one of the many ways businesses suffer at the hands of con artists and unscrupulous consumers. While the Department of Justice does not estimate dollar losses in crimes practiced on cashiers, its experience indicates that at some time virtually every business that transacts goods or services through a cashier or sales clerk will be victimized.

The list of crimes commonly practiced on cashiers or sales clerks includes:

- Quick-change scams
- Currency switches
- Counterfeit bill passing
- Price tag switches
- Container switches
- Refund and exchange fraud

 PROTECT YOUR BUSINESS

As is often the case in crimes practiced on retail businesses, the merchant's most effective recourse—indeed, sometimes the only recourse—is a staff aware of the methods of con artists and trained in recognizing and circumventing their schemes.

The Scheme

Quick change artists are criminals well-versed in the art of fast talking. Typically, the con artist will bring a small purchase to the cashier and offer to pay with a large denomination bill. As the cashier hands over the proper change, the con artist "discovers" that he has a smaller denomination bill and withdraws the large bill. With his hands already on the change, he attempts, through a rapid exchange of money, to confuse the cashier into believing that the correct amount of money has changed hands. In reality, the con artist ends up walking away with all of the change from the small bill *plus* all or part of the change issued on the larger denomination.

Your Defense

The best defense against a quick-change artist is an alert, cautious, "street-wise" cashier who understands the importance of taking time and not becoming rattled when money is being transacted.

The cash register should be well out of the reach of customers so a con artist cannot "assist" the cashier in making change. When the cashier rings up a sale, she should take the bill from the customer and place it on a safe but open spot away from the open cash drawer. The customer's money *should not* be immediately placed in the cash drawer.

The cashier should count out the change at least twice, once to herself and a second time to the customer. If the customer attempts to exchange a smaller bill for the original large bill, the cashier should retrieve the change she was about to give the customer, return it to the cash register, and start over with the new bill. Until the sale has been completed, the customer's and cash register's money should not be mingled.

If the cashier becomes confused, she should close the cash drawer immediately and call for the store manager to assist in the transaction. Speed and confusion are the quick-change artist's allies—when complications develop, he will usually abandon the scam.

The Scheme

Currency switches are a form of counterfeiting, which is a federal offense. In most cases the con artist will attempt to pay for a purchase with a bill that has been tampered with so that it appears to be of a higher denomination. For example, the con artist may hand over a bogus $20 bill that is actually a $1 bill. The illusion can be most convincing.

Typically, the con artist will take a number of $20 bills (or bills of another high denomination) and clip the numerical value from one corner of each bill. (The mutilated bills with three corners are still negotiable.) The clipped corners are then pasted over the corners of $1 bills and the edges sanded to blend color and texture. Some con artists apply the fake corners to only one side of the bill, hoping the cashier will not examine the other side.

Your Defense

Cashiers should be alerted to the practice of currency switches and trained to examine bills quickly for counterfeits. A cursory examination of the look and feel of the corners of high-denomination bills, plus a glance to confirm that the correct face is pictured, should be sufficient to spot the imposters.

☐ ══════════════════════════════════════ ☐

COUNTERFEITING

Counterfeiting of money is one of the oldest crimes in history. It was a serious problem in the early days of our country when banks issued their own currency. By the time of the Civil War, it was estimated that one-third of all currency in circulation was counterfeit.

At that time, there were approximately 1,600 state banks designing and printing their own notes. Each note carried a different design, making it difficult to distinguish the 4,000 varieties of counterfeits from the 7,000 varieties of genuine notes.

It was hoped the adoption of a national currency in 1863 would solve the counterfeiting problem. However, the national currency was soon counterfeited so extensively it became necessary for the government to take enforcement measures. Therefore, on July 5, 1865, the United States Secret Service was established to suppress counterfeiting.

Counterfeiting has been substantially curtailed since the establishment of the Secret Service. But in this century, modern photographic and printing devices have made the production of counterfeit money relatively easy.

You can help protect your business from this threat by becoming more familiar with United States currency.

Characteristics of United States Paper Currency

There are three types or classes of U.S. paper currency in circulation. The name of each class appears on the upper face of the bill. The different class bills are further identified by the color of their Treasury Seal and Serial Numbers.

CLASS	COLOR OF TREASURY SEAL AND SERIAL NUMBER	DENOMINATION
Federal Reserve Notes	Green	$1, $2, $5, $10, $20, $50, and $100
United States Notes	Red	$2, $5, and $100
Silver Certificates	Blue	$1, $5, and $10

Each denomination, regardless of class, has a prescribed portrait and back design, selected by the Secretary of the Treasury and the Secretary's advisors.

Notes of the $500, $1,000, $5,000, and $10,000 denomination have not been printed for many years and are being removed from circulation. The portraits appearing on these notes are: McKinley on the $500, Cleveland on the $1,000, Madison on the $5,000, and Chase* on the $10,000.

Portraits and Back Designs on Paper Currency

$1
George Washington
Great Seal of the United States

$2
Thomas Jefferson
Declaration of Independence

$5
Abraham Lincoln
Lincoln Memorial

$10
Alexander Hamilton
U.S. Treasury Building

$20
Andrew Jackson
White House

$50
Ulysses S. Grant
U.S. Capitol

$100
Benjamin Franklin
Independence Hall

Design Features Which Vary on Genuine Currency

Signature
Design features sometimes vary from one series year to another. The most common variance comes with changes in the identity, and

*Salmon Portland Chase (1808-73) was secretary of the treasury from 1861-64, during which period he created a national bank system.

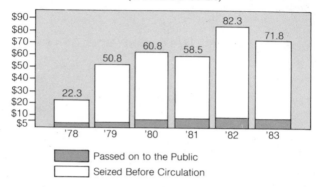

COUNTERFEITING TREND$
Counterfeit Notes
(in millions of dollars)

Passed on to the Public
Seized Before Circulation

therefore the signature, of the Secretary of the Treasury or the Treasurer of the United States.

Treasury Seal
The 1963B series marked a change in note design. One dollar Federal Reserve Notes of that series year featured a redesigned Treasury seal with an English inscription instead of a Latin one. The new seal, phased in over succeeding years, appears on all notes of the 1969 series year or later.

Motto
"In God We Trust" first appeared on the $1 Silver Certificate of the 1957 series year. It was gradually phased in thereafter on other denominations and classes and is printed on the back of all U.S. paper currency of the series year 1963 or later.

Serial Numbers and Star Notes
Each note has its own individual series number. When a note is mutilated in the course of manufacture, it must be replaced in the series to ensure a proper count of the notes produced. To print another note with an identical serial number would be costly and time-con-

suming. Consequently, a "star note" is substituted. This note has a serial number which is out of sequence with the others in the series. A star is printed after the number to show that it was placed in series as a substitute. A "star note" is also used for the 100,000,000th note in a series.

Federal Reserve Seal

Each Federal Reserve Note bears a regional seal at the left of the portrait. This seal, printed in black, bears the name of the issuing Federal Reserve Bank and the letter designating the Federal Reserve district in which that bank is located. On notes of the 1950 series and later, the black Federal Reserve regional seal is smaller than earlier designs and is surrounded by sharp points.

Jackson Portrait

Another commonly noticed design inconsistency occurs in the portrait of Andrew Jackson on the $20 note. In the 1934 and 1950 series, he is depicted with one more finger showing than on notes of other series years.

Check Letter, Face Plate Number, Back Plate Number, Quadrant Number

These designations are printed in various specific locations on the note. They are used by the Bureau of Engraving and Printing in the manufacturing process.

Recognizing the Counterfeit Bill

The best method of detecting a counterfeit bill is to compare the suspect note with a genuine bill of the same denomination and series, paying attention to the quality of printing and paper characteristics. *Look for differences, not similarities.*

Examine the tiny red and blue *fibers* imbedded in the paper of a genuine note. It is illegal to reproduce this distinctive paper. Often counterfeiters try to simulate these fibers by printing tiny red and blue lines on their paper. Close inspection reveals, however, that on the counterfeit the lines are printed on the surface, not imbedded in the paper.

Notice the *workmanship* of the note's design. Genuine money is made by the government's master craftsmen using expensive steel engraving and printing equipment designed for that purpose. Most

GENUINE   COUNTERFEIT

(Genuine plate
makes clear lines)

(Counterfeit plate
makes broken lines)

counterfeiters use a photo-mechanical, or "offset" method to make a printing plate from a photograph of a genuine note. The resulting product looks flat and lacks fine detail.

Further, the lines in the portrait background, if you look closely, form squares. On counterfeits, some of these squares may be filled in, and many of the delicate lines in the portrait may be broken or missing.

Some people believe that a bill must be counterfeit if the ink rubs off. This is not true. Genuine currency, when rubbed on paper, can leave ink smears.

Source: United States Secret Service

☐ ══ ☐

The Scheme

In the early 1950s, sticky backed price tags came into widespread use and *price tag switches* joined the petty thief's bag of tricks. Con artists could discreetly peel off price tags and replace them with lower priced tags while the merchandise was still on the shelf. The stamping of merchandise with prices in ink proved no more reliable an alternative. Con artists equipped with handkerchiefs soaked in ink remover could simply wipe the price off an item and give the cashier an inaccurate price. Another common ploy targeted primarily at grocery stores involves the switching of the ticketed lids of containers of similar products. For example, the plastic top of an expensive can of coffee can be switched with the top from a less expensive can before the item is brought to the cashier.

Your Defense

The increasing use of UPC codes stamped directly on product packages is the most effective deterrent to price tag switching. In stores where price tags must still be used, managers should ensure that the tags are affixed in a manner that makes them removable only by the cashier or only by being destroyed. On clothing, for example, garment tags affixed with plastic loops can be removed only by breaking the loop, and once the loop is broken the tags cannot be easily reattached. For putting prices directly on merchandise, sticky backed labels are available that rip when removed and consequently cannot be reused.

Also effective, though expensive, is the use of electronic cash terminals hooked up with a central computer that contains current price information filed under stock numbers. Where cost makes the installation of these terminals impractical, it's a good idea to provide cashiers with current lists of sale items and prices. Cashiers should become familiar with these prices and should refer to the lists frequently.

The Scheme

Container switches and price tag switches are closely related. In a container switch, the con artist removes the contents from a ticketed container and refills the container with a similar, but higher-priced, item. A shirt, for example, may be removed from its plastic bag and placed in a bag that originally contained a less expensive shirt.

In a variation of the container switch, the con artist opens a bag, box, or other container and conceals another item inside. A small, expensive toy, for example, may be hidden inside a box containing a less expensive toy, such as a model with numerous pieces. In grocery stores where customers bag their own produce, the container switch is a recurring and pervasive problem, with customers concealing expensive produce in bags of less costly items.

Your Defense

Retail managers should make sure that product containers are tightly sealed and that when containers with broken seals are presented for purchase, they are first opened and their contents examined. In grocery stores, cashiers should be made aware of the container switch and should be able to identify the different types of produce. Groceries should use transparent plastic bags for produce, and cashiers should be instructed to habitually shake and check bags to be certain that other items haven't been mixed in with less costly produce.

The Scheme

Refund and exchange fraud comes in many forms, including the following common schemes.

- Merchandise is shoplifted and then returned for a refund or exchange.

- A shoplifter collects discarded sales receipts, "lifts" items priced at the amounts shown on the salvaged receipts, and then returns the items, with receipts, for refund.

- An article is purchased by check; the customer stops payment on the check and before the check bounces, returns the article for a refund. (Also see Chapter 11, Check Fraud.)

- Merchandise that was broken or damaged by a customer is repackaged and returned for exchange, refund, or credit.

- An item purchased at one store is returned for credit to another store that sells the same item at a higher price.

Your Defense

Some stores do not allow merchandise returns or exchanges, but most find that offering at least one or all of the three basic options—refund, exchange, and credit—is an important part of a good customer relations policy.

We recommend that every business set a uniform returns policy based at least in part on the policies of the store's suppliers and on the local and state laws that govern refunds, exchanges, returns, warranties, and service contracts. Policies should be simple, understandable, and consistent, and should be posted in a prominent location, such as over each cash register. Sales receipts, too, should carry a printed explanation of the store's refund/exchange policy. In some states and localities, consumer protection laws specify the acceptable manner of posting of merchants' refund and exchange policies.

Return policies should stipulate that, to return merchandise, the customer must have a cash register or credit card receipt as proof of purchase and that the merchandise must be in resalable condition, unless defects resulted from inferior product quality, not misuse by the customer.

On the return of high-priced items, many stores require that the refund be credited to the customer's charge account or that a refund check be sent to the customer's home address.

Exchange policies also should cover only merchandise that is in a condition to be resold or that contains defects for which the customer cannot be held responsible, and should require at minimum a sales receipt, cash register receipt, canceled check, or other proof of purchase. There have been numerous cases of criminals purchasing bulk shipments of damaged or defective goods at a fraction of retail costs, and returning the items for credit or exchanging them for non-defective products.

Returns for credit should require that merchandise be returned within a specified time period. Con artists have been known to purchase bulk quantities of out-of-date or no longer stylish items at greatly reduced prices, only to return them for credit or refund.

 ## IF YOU ARE VICTIMIZED

When the schemes described here are practiced on cashiers and are detected only after the fact, the merchant has little or no recourse. Even when a suspect is caught "in the act," there is little the merchant can do beyond preventing losses by shortcircuiting the scheme.

In cases involving currency switches and counterfeiting, the cashier who is offered the bill should attempt to stall the suspect while the police or U.S. Secret Service are contacted. Note the suspect's description, the description of any companions, and the description and license number of any vehicle used. The cashier should initial and date the bill, and it should be placed in a protective cover and handed over to the police or Secret Service.

CHAPTER 9

A CASE OF

Sticky Fingers

After taking a physical inventory, the owner of a bustling grocery store concludes that shoplifting is reducing his revenues by several hundred dollars each week. Aware that some area stores use convex mirrors placed in out-of-the-way spots to enable employees to keep an eye on potential shoplifters, the grocer decides to invest in several of these mirrors.

For several weeks after the mirrors are installed, shoplifting seems to subside. But within a few months, the incidence of pilferage reaches new heights. Determining that an even greater investment in

Shoplifting

his store's security is needed, the owner hires a uniformed security guard to walk the aisles. The impact is much the same—shoplifting subsides for a few weeks and then returns to previous levels.

Faced with the prospect of adding other, even more costly shoplifting deterrents, such as closed circuit television or plain-clothes security guards, the resigned store owner concludes that it will be more cost-effective simply to allow the problem to continue and write off shoplifting losses as a cost of doing business.

Perpetrator Profiles

Shoplifting has been estimated to cost American business between $8 billion and $16 billion annually, but these figures, says the U.S. Department of Justice, and any other attempts to estimate the dollars lost in shoplifting vary dramatically and are at best "rough estimates" because in the majority of cases, the crime of shoplifting goes undetected.

Shoplifting occurs primarily on the sales floors or at the check-out counters of retail stores. On the sales floor, nonprofessional shoplifters steal goods that can be quickly and easily hidden inside clothing, a backpack, or a pocketbook. Professional shoplifters—those for whom crime is a primary source of income—are much more skillful. Cleverly disguised devices, such as clothing specially designed with large hidden pockets or parcels with hidden "drop-out" compartments, help the pro conceal items both small and large.

At the check-out counter, shoplifting may occur when otherwise honest customers become disgruntled at having to wait in inordinately slow lines. "I wanted to pay for the item," the customer may rationalize, "but the store was too inefficient to collect my money." Other normally honest customers who wheel out stolen goods on the bottom shelves of grocery carts may justify their actions by reasoning that, after all, they presented the items at the checkout counter—it was the checker who failed to do his or her job properly.

The Mechanics of Prevention

For many years, businesses have employed a number of protective devices and measures to try to detect and reduce shoplifting. Electronic sensing devices, closed circuit television, convex mirrors, uniformed and plain-clothes security guards, observation mirrors, and warning signs are among the more commonly used deterrents.

As part of a comprehensive, ever-changing program, these systems may prove effective in reducing the incidence of shoplifting. But, say many law enforcement authorities, there are more effective approaches. "Psychological deterrents" designed to make potential shoplifters feel uncomfortable and insecure about their actions are not only more effective, but their overall cost is usually minimal when compared to the costs involved with the mechanical or labor-intensive methods.

The following brief overview of various psychological and mechanical deterrents may help business owners determine which combination may best suit their particular situation. We also urge you to contact your local police department for information on state laws concerning shoplifting and procedures to follow to prevent the crime.

PROTECT YOUR BUSINESS

Psychological Deterrents

☐ **Keep displays neat** by arranging products in rows rather than in disorganized piles. When a display is organized, it is easier to spot when something is missing.

☐ **Service-oriented establishments should instruct employees to greet customers as they enter the store** and to ask if they may be of service. Shoplifters generally dislike being spoken to while they are "working," and personal attention often so un-nerves them that they will leave without committing a crime.

☐ **Require customers to "check" packages and other containers while shopping.** In grocery stores, prevent concealment of stolen items beneath produce by using clear plastic bags.

☐ **Be alert in distracting situations.** Professional shoplifters often work in pairs. One will create a disturbance, such as an "accident" or argument, and while employees are distracted, the other will make off with the goods.

☐ **Show customers only one valuable item at a time.** A flimflam artist can easily slip a small item into a sleeve or pocket. Also, never allow display cases to remain unlocked while unattended.

☐ **"High-risk" merchandise**—electronic equipment, leather coats, and other items known to be particularly attractive to shoplifters—should be displayed behind counters, in locked cases, or on chained racks.

☐ **Arrange the store so that everyone leaving must pass a checkout counter.** Check the bottom of shopping carts, and, if possible, speak with customers as they leave. If a cashier suspects that someone is leaving the store with a concealed item, a question such as "May I help you with your purchase?" will unnerve a shoplifter without incriminating the employee if no shoplifting has occurred. (Also see Chapter 8, Crimes Practiced on Cashiers.)

☐ **Cut down on the number of exits.** A store with many exits makes it easy for a shoplifter to slip out with merchandise. If compliance with local fire laws is a problem, exits may be converted to emergency exits.

☐ **Consider an employee training program.** Local law enforcement officials may be able to help you to set up a program for training employees in identifying potential shoplifters, approaching them without unlawfully accusing them, and, if necessary, preventing them from leaving with stolen goods. The emphasis in a training program should be on preventing the crime, rather than on surveillance with the intent of apprehending the criminal. In any case, employees should not be asked to apprehend shoplifting suspects.

Protective Devices and Systems

☐ **Signs that warn against shoplifting** have mixed results. In some instances, these signs, which usually contain a description of state laws against shoplifting, may help to scare off some young offenders. But more experienced offenders seem to ignore the signs, and some reports indicate that the incidence of shoplifting actually increases after signs are put in place.

☐ **Convex mirrors** that expose hard-to-see corners of the store have limited success as deterrents. While the mirrors allow employees to keep an eye on suspected shoplifters, they also allow shoplifters to watch employees—and when the employee isn't looking, the crime is committed.

☐ **Uniformed guards** often prove effective at first, but once professional shoplifters have had time to observe and adapt to the guards' habits, the deterrence factor diminishes. Stationary guards posted at all exits are most effective.

☐ **Plain-clothes guards** seem to be more effective than uniformed guards in the apprehension of shoplifters. They have the advantage of being able to stay close to suspected offenders; once professional shoplifters ascertain their identity, however, plain-clothes guards lose this advantage.

☐ **Balcony office areas** equipped with one-way mirrors and used as observation posts by management or security personnel are expensive to operate on a full-time basis, but have proven effective in identifying and deterring shoplifters.

☐ **Peepholes** also are costly to operate, but they may be used effectively in specific problem areas.

☐ **Closed-circuit television cameras** are coming into increasing use and have often proven effective. While television cameras have had success in deterring nonprofessional offenders, some law enforcement authorities caution that professionals may react

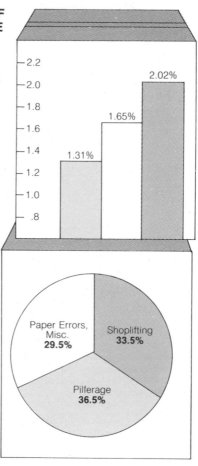

PERCENTAGE OF SALES REVENUE LOST DUE TO STOCK SHORTAGES IN RETAIL STORES IN 1983

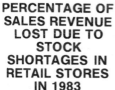 Specialty Stores

☐ Stores w/sales $1 million–$5 million

▨ Stores w/sales over $5 million

2.2
2.0
1.8
1.6
1.4
1.2
1.0
.8

1.31%

1.65%

2.02%

1983 RETAIL STOCK SHORTAGES BY CAUSE

Paper Errors, Misc. **29.5%**

Shoplifting **33.5%**

Pilferage **36.5%**

Source: National Retail Merchants Association

105

to them in the same way they do to uniformed guards—by learning how to commit the offense out of view. Some retailers hold down costs by installing impressive-looking, effective deterrent systems that use both genuine cameras and "dummies."

☐ **Electronic sensing devices** are the latest, most expensive, and most effective of the deterrent systems. Most electronic tags are attached to merchandise in a manner that makes their removal nearly impossible without the proper equipment. Other "invisible" tags must be deactivated by being passed over a device at the checkout counter. Sensors are placed by store exits, and if tagged merchandise passes a sensor, an alarm sounds. While an effective deterrent, the system has its potential drawbacks—if a cashier neglects to remove or deactivate the electronic device when an item is purchased and the customer then sets off the alarm, the merchant who accuses the innocent shopper of theft may be subject to a civil suit. Some retailers alleviate this problem by positioning trained employees near the sensors during high traffic periods.

 IF YOU ARE VICTIMIZED

Laws against shoplifting differ in each of the 50 states and are continually changing. We recommend that you contact your state or local police department for up-to-date information on the laws of your own state. Also follow these basic guidelines.

- If you are certain a customer has concealed an article on his or her person with the intention of leaving the store without paying for it, your actions should be aimed at inducing the individual to either purchase or return the item. For example, you might ask, "May I ring that up for you?"

- A voluntary approach, if at all possible, is always preferable. If a suspect voluntarily remains in the store or accompanies a store official to an office to discuss the matter, issues of false imprisonment generally are not involved.

- Most state laws permit merchants to open customers' packages only when they are certain those packages contain concealed items. Merchants may not "frisk" customers or inspect packages at random, and by law, they may not search a suspect unless that individual has been placed under arrest.

- While some state laws permit a merchant to apprehend a suspect if that individual has concealed an item and then left the department, it is generally considered advisable to wait until the suspect has left the store with the merchandise.

- In some states and in the District of Columbia, shoplifting includes some instances of price tag and container switches. (See Chapter 8, Crimes Practiced on Cashiers.)

- If you are certain someone has left your store with a concealed article, you may choose to swear out a warrant for the suspect's arrest. Unfortunately, unless you can positively prove that the article was stolen from your store, it is unlikely that this action will result in the return of the stolen goods or prosecution of the suspected shoplifter.

CHAPTER 10

THE CASE OF

The Artful Chargers

A chain of drugstores features an eight-page "dollar days" circular in Sunday's edition of the local newspaper. That Sunday, thousands of cost-conscious shoppers jam the stores, creating long lines at the check-out counters.

The cashiers, many of whom are high-school students working weekends, feel the pressure of the lines of impatient customers. To several of the newer employees, one of the most tedious and time-consuming impediments to ringing up sales quickly is the need to look up credit card numbers. Card recovery bulletins listing "hot numbers" are provided weekly by the various credit card issuers; the numbers represent accounts which for one reason or another are considered invalid. The stores' managers have always emphasized the importance of checking card expiration dates and customer signatures and looking through the list for "hot numbers." Nevertheless, faced with an endless stream of harried shoppers, some of the

Credit Card Fraud

equally harried checkers save time by making only a cursory flip through the pages or even bypassing the check altogether.

At the end of the day, each store sends copies of all credit card slips to its bank and to the main office. The results of carelessness are soon revealed—when the banks notify the chain's main office that a number of fraudulent purchases have slipped through. Because specified procedures were not followed, those hundreds of dollars worth of purchases will not be reimbursed by the credit card issuers. Each store will attempt to recover payment from its customers, but in the end, a significant portion of the fraudulent buys will be chalked up as lost revenues.

The Credit Card Revolution

According to the Fraud and Theft Information Bureau, the purchasing power, or combined credit limits, of all credit cards in the United States equals twice the value of all currency in circulation. This purchasing power is spread out over about 600 million credit cards, with 116 million Americans holding at least one card, and most having several.

The Committee on Banking, Finance and Urban Affairs of the U.S. Congress reports that in the early 1980s, seventy-three million credit cards were lost or stolen each year, and of that total some twenty thousand credit cards were fraudulently used each day. Losses are high—the average loss incurred from a stolen card is $650; from a counterfeit card, $1,102. Estimates of total losses—including bank losses, losses in merchandise and services by merchants, and consumer losses—ranged as high as $3 billion in 1984. These losses have been increasing at a staggering rate. Worldwide credit card industry losses from counterfeit cards alone jumped 330 percent from 1981 to '82, for instance, with 94 percent of those losses in the United States.

Banks, department stores, and oil companies that issue credit cards all feel the brunt of these financial losses. The American Bank-

CONSUMER CREDIT HELD BY RETAILERS REACHED $61.9 BILLION IN 1983

Percentage of Department Store Sales* by Terms of Sale

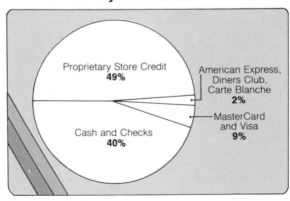

Proprietary Store Credit
49%

American Express, Diners Club, Carte Blanche
2%

MasterCard and Visa
9%

Cash and Checks
40%

*average of median figures

Source: *Retail Credit Operating Results 1983*
National Retail Merchants Association

ers Association, which closely monitors credit card losses by its member banks, estimates that the average loss per bank has sky-rocketed from over $700 thousand in 1979 to nearly $13 million in 1982. Affected businesses include not only the nation's retailers, but also restaurants, hotels, airlines, travel agents, car rental companies, mail-order companies, and other businesses that cannot survive without accepting credit cards.

But it is the consumer who ultimately picks up the tab. One major credit card company estimated in 1983 that fraud losses cost the system about eight cents per transaction, a 900 percent increase from 1971. This cost is necessarily reflected in the prices charged consumers. Further, consumers are liable for up to $50 of unautho-rized charges per card if their cards are lost or stolen and the credit card issuer is not notified before the charges are made.

A Cache of Thieves

Perpetrators of credit card fraud—the illegal use of stolen or counter-feit credit cards—fit no one mold. From seemingly honest merchants to underworld figures, they each have their own peculiar method of operation. The con artist commonly will use the stolen or counterfeit

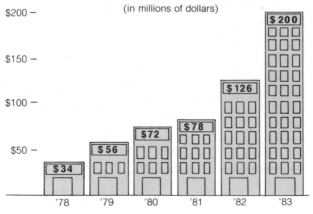

CREDIT CARD FRAUD:

Total Bank Losses From Counterfeit or Altered Cards

(in millions of dollars)

Source: American Bankers Association

card for only a few days and then discard it, but even that practice varies. The following thumbnail sketches profile several "typical" credit card criminals.

A youth spends several weeks traveling across the country, living off purchases made on credit cards found in a wallet stolen from the front seat of a car.

Racketeers steal legitimate but blank credit cards and imprint them with the names and numbers of active accounts, obtained from cooperative merchants or discarded credit card carbon slips. The new cards are sold to underworld contacts, who use other forged identification papers to operate a long-term scheme to bilk the credit card issuer and area businesses.

A small-time hustler makes his living "ironing" the numbers, names, and expiration dates off stolen credit cards and selling newly imprinted cards to other con artists.

A team of underworld loansharks acquires legitimate businesses and pushes them into insolvency; a key part of their scheme involves running the companies' credit cards to their spending limits before filing for bankruptcy. (See Chapter 5 for further details on Bankruptcy Fraud.)

A merchant cooperates with a counterfeiter by using plain plastic cards embossed with active account numbers to imprint phony sales slips, which are then sent to the bank for collection.

An individual searches through a restaurant's trash for carbons from used credit card forms and uses the numbers to charge merchandise over the phone or by mail.

 ## PROTECT YOUR BUSINESS

Credit card issuers are fighting back with concerted efforts to develop techniques that eventually will stem the dramatic rise in credit card fraud. Among the most heralded improvements are new counterfeitproof, tamperproof cards that will contain holographic, or three-dimensional, images; fine-line printing; ultraviolet inks; and microprinted Bank Identification Numbers (BINs).

Even with these advancements, experts say, the only truly effective solution will be the electronic identification of each customer and authorization of every transaction at the point of sale. Electronic identification should be a reality by 1990. But, say the experts, there are

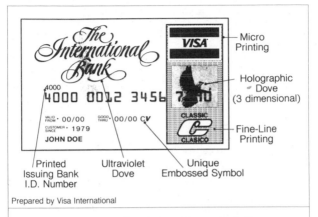

Micro Printing

Holographic Dove (3 dimensional)

Fine-Line Printing

Printed Issuing Bank I.D. Number

Ultraviolet Dove

Unique Embossed Symbol

Prepared by Visa International

Turning the Cards on Counterfeiters

Several properties designed to make counterfeiting more difficult have been incorporated in a new design for all Visa cards. Conversion to the new design will be completed by late 1986. The properties include:

- a dove, a Visa service mark, reproduced as a rainbow hologram over the last four digits of the account number

- a second dove, visible only under ultraviolet light, in the center of the card

- micro-printed bank identification codes

- a field of fine-line printing

- an embossed security symbol

- a printed BIN above the embossed number

The new cards highlight the name of the bank issuing the card, rather than Visa. MasterCard also is phasing in redesigned cards that incorporate similar security properties.

a number of actions today's merchants can take to combat credit card fraud.

Screening all purchases and stopping fraudulent transactions before they occur remains the best precautionary strategy. Most major credit card issuers establish a "floor limit" (usually $50); retail transactions over that amount require telephone authorization. For purchases under the limit, the merchant may complete the transaction, but only by first verifying that the card's expiration date hasn't been reached, the customer's signature matches that on the card, and the account number is not listed in the card recovery bulletin. The merchant who completes a questionable transaction without performing these checks may be held responsible for any resulting losses. In any case, *merchants should be on the lookout for:*

- Altered, expired, or not-yet-valid credit cards

- Signatures that do not match on the card and sales slip

- Cards that do not register imprints on carbon copies

- Customers who make numerous small credit card purchases, all under the amount at which an authorization call to the card issuer is required

- Impatient applicants for department store credit cards who use impressive names or titles to try to hasten the approval process

Merchants can reduce the likelihood of credit card fraud by:

- Using electronic authorization terminals, calling credit card issuers for authorization on all card purchases, or conducting random authorization checks on small purchases.

- Requiring a valid photo identification for acceptance of credit card purchases.

- Copying the name, address, and phone number of every credit card customer from the photo I.D., and then asking the authorization center to verify that information.

- Keeping a list of local bank telephone numbers near each cash register and checking local card BINs with the issuing bank. After banking hours, call your telephone directory assistance which will not *provide* addresses, but will *verify* given addresses.

- Checking carbon copies to be certain that clear imprints have been made. The carbon paper, which also contains the imprint of the credit card number, should be destroyed, or merchants should use carbonless-type receipts or perforated carbons that split after use.

While some of these preventative measures might seem time-consuming, the extra efforts have proven effective deterrents to credit card crime. When they see such precautions being taken to clear their credit purchases, swindlers often choose to pay cash or cancel the transaction altogether. A store can build the enviable reputation of being difficult, if not impossible, to swindle.

 # IF YOU ARE VICTIMIZED

Credit cards are the property of their issuing companies. Those who legally carry and use credit cards do so with the permission and authorization of the issuer. Therefore, a credit card company will instruct a merchant who is presented with a card that is being used in an unauthorized manner to refuse to allow the purchase and often will further authorize the merchant to confiscate the card. Most issuing institutions emphasize the importance of the merchant's attempt to retain the card and thus prevent its further illegal use, but they also caution that an effort should be made to confiscate a card only if it seems reasonably safe to do so. If not, the merchant should try to discreetly copy the card's account and Bank Identification Numbers, and any other pertinent information (the suspect's name, address, driver's license number, etc.) before returning the card.

Police authorities recommend that a merchant stall an individual using a stolen or counterfeit card for as long as possible *without resorting to physical detention*. While the suspect is "waiting for verification of the card," the merchant or cashier should inconspicuously telephone the police. If the suspect insists on leaving before the police arrive, the merchant should try to get a license number and description of the car or other vehicle used. A detailed description of the suspect and any companions, and an indication of the direction taken by car or on foot, also will be helpful to the police.

While credit card fraud is a federal crime and violators can and should be prosecuted, merchants who suffer losses by not following stipulated verification procedures may have difficulty recovering lost funds. Some credit card issuers may agree to reimburse some initial losses, but businesses that frequently bypass the transaction verification procedure may be forced to cover their own losses.

CHAPTER 11

The Friendly Forger

A well-dressed woman visits a gift shop and seeks out the store manager. She is visiting family in the area, is shopping for gifts, and has run out of cash. It is Saturday and the banks are closed, so she is hoping the merchant will allow her to pay for her purchase with an out-of-state check, made out for $50 over the purchase price so she can buy a few items elsewhere.

The manager is sympathetic. If she can provide some identification, he will be glad to help her. The woman presents several credit cards, from which he carefully copies the numbers. As an added precaution, he also asks for the local address of the woman's relatives. The purchase is made and the check cashed.

Check Fraud

On Monday the check is deposited; on Wednesday the manager receives a call from his bank. The check is no good—the signature has been forged and, it turns out, the check comes from a checkbook stolen a week earlier along with several credit cards and various personal possessions.

The merchant is forced to absorb the $50 cash and $25 purchase. The woman's ''local address'' does not exist, and she is never found.

Quiet but Costly

Schemes involving the passing of bad checks have always figured among the most prevalent forms of crime against banks and businesses. The U.S. Department of Justice estimated in 1976 that, with an average per-check loss of $72, the passing of bad checks cost banks and businesses over $4.7 million per day, or $1.7 billion per year. By 1984, says one Department spokesman, that $1.7 billion figure had more than doubled.

Virtually any type of check, whether written for the payment of a bill, a federal or state tax refund, a payroll, welfare benefits, or the purchase of goods or services, can be fraudulently redeemed. The four most common types of bad checks are:

1. **Checks drawn on insufficient funds.** An individual or business issues a check—intentionally or unknowingly—on a bank account without the funds to cover it.

BAD CHECK LOSSES
Percentage of Department Store Sales Volume Lost Due to Bad Checks 1979–83

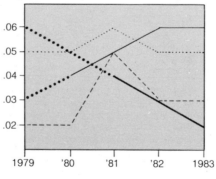

..... Figures not available
——— Sales under $20 million
▬▬▬ Sales $20 million–$100 million
－－－ Sales $100 million–$250 million
·········· Sales over $250 million

Source: *Retail Credit Operating Results 1983*
National Retail Merchants Association

2. **Completely falsified checks.** The person passing the check may have fabricated or printed it and usually forges the signatures and endorsements. These checks are often drawn on bank accounts that are nonexistent or defunct—sometimes even the bank identified on the check is nonexistent.

3. **Legitimate checks that have been falsified.** Legitimate checks, already filled out and signed, are stolen from homes, offices, or the mail, and are then altered or forged. The amount of the legitimate check can be increased by altering a figure or adding a zero.

4. **Checks falsified on legitimate bank accounts.** These include stolen blank checks and high-quality photocopies or other reproductions of legitimate blank checks. The swindler fills out the check, forging the signature of the account holder.

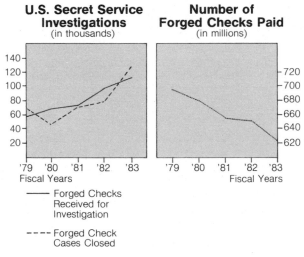

CHECK FORGERY
Fiscal Years 1979–1983

Source: United States Secret Service

Check fraud is a "silent" crime—the store owner or employee who accepts a bad check usually doesn't even realize a crime has been committed until the bank in which the check is deposited reports one of the following.

- The account on which the check is drawn has funds insufficient to cover it. The payee usually can attempt to redeposit the check at a later date, but if the second attempt also fails, the check generally is canceled by the bank and the payee must seek recourse through other channels.

- It has no account corresponding with the account number on the check deposited. Subsequent investigation usually reveals a completely falsified check.

- The check has been drawn on a closed bank account. While this may be the result of carelessness on the part of the checkwriter, in cases of fraud the writer usually will have passed numerous checks on an account opened and then closed for the purpose of conducting the fraud.

Case Histories in Brief

The following are only a few examples of the many variations of check fraud.

☐ A dishonest employee or other individual gains access to a company's checkwriting machine and executive signature imprinter. This equipment is used to make up seemingly legitimate checks on the company's account, with checks often taken from the back of the checkbook so their absence will not be immediately noticed.

☐ A bad check—either completely falsified or drawn on a legitimate account with insufficient funds—is sent as payment for a mail-order purchase. By the time the check "bounces," the order has been received and the recipient has vanished.

☐ The recipient—whether legitimate or unintended —of a check increases its face value by altering or adding to existing numbers and wording.

☐ Con artists create a phony company that pays other legitimate businesses with fraudulent checks drawn on insufficient funds or nonexistent bank accounts. Many businesses will provide goods or services and accept checks as payment from another business, even one previously unknown, without verifying that the company actually exists.

☐ A "customer" presents a stolen or fraudulent check at a check cashing window or grocery store. Often these checks are "paid" toward a purchase, inducing the merchant to cash the check in order to make the sale.

☐ Bogus payroll checks are cashed on payday at the bank at which the company that supposedly issued them maintains its payroll account.

☐ Stolen travelers checks are redeemed, usually with no identification required.

PROTECT YOUR BUSINESS

Businesses that establish, maintain, and advertise firm check cashing policies generally have few problems with bad checks. The following precautions make effective guidelines in a policy aimed at combatting check fraud.

1. **Always insist on proper identification.** The check should be imprinted with the customer's name and address, and the customer should have a valid driver's license with a recent photograph and a major credit card. But remember that if the check was stolen, credit cards, Social Security cards, and other forms of identification also may have been taken.

2. **Examine the check carefully.** The extra effort involved in carefully scrutinizing every check can pay off. When the check is presented to you directly, insist that it be written and signed in front of you. Don't be misled into assuming that a check made out on a checkwriting machine or typewriter is legitimate.

   Be cautious about accepting checks that contain oddly shaped, possibly altered, numerals; variations in ink color or thicknesses of lines or letters; erasures, whited-out sections, or unusual spacing; ink that appears to have been traced over pencil; and endorsement signatures that differ from the signature on the front of the check.

   Also be wary of:

   • Signatures that appear out of character for the individual cashing the check, such as a small, precise feminine signature from a young boy or large man. When in doubt, ask the person to sign again in front of you, and watch how he or she signs.

- Individuals who take extreme caution and much time signing their names.

- Customers who try to distract you while they are signing the check or you are examining it.

3. **Always verify certified checks.** Checks that indicate that their validity has been certified by a bank can be forged. Do not hesitate to call the bank for verification. If you cannot contact the bank and you have serious doubts about the check's validity, refuse to accept the check. And with a personal or business check, insist on identification with a photo and signature.

4. **All "traveler's checks" are not necessarily legitimate.** Check fraud artists know that many merchants believe that even stolen traveler's checks will be redeemed by the issuing companies. In fact, in most cases, the major traveler's check companies will honor stolen traveler's checks that have been unknowingly accepted by a merchant. But if the endorsement of the stolen check does not closely resemble the authorized signature, the check issuer may refuse to redeem the check. If in doubt, merchants can refuse to accept the check or can request valid photo identification and record identification data on the check. Also, be wary of situations in which many traveler's checks are cashed at one time.

    Do not accept traveler's checks that have been endorsed in advance. Require another signature while you watch.

5. **Safeguard your business and personal checkbooks and checkwriting equipment.** Also place bank statements and canceled checks in a safe location.

6. **Allow personal checks to be cashed with purchases only,** and require that they be made out for the exact amount of the purchase.

7. **Do not accept "stale" checks,** particularly those that are more than two weeks old. Request that checks be made out with the date of purchase, or, if that is not possible, contact the customer's bank for verification.

8. **Do not accept second-party checks.**

9. **Set a reasonable dollar limit on checks.** This should be based on what is considered an average purchase in your business. For example, a bowling alley should not cash checks for $50 if the average customer pays only $5.

10. **Consider the use of check cashing cards,** which may be offered to customers after an initial credit check with local banks and credit checking agencies.

11. **Don't accept postdated checks,** except in cases where a customer leaves a deposit on goods or services to be received at a later date. If a customer admits to having insufficient funds to cover the check and offers a postdated check under the condition that the money will be deposited in the account at a later date, insist on another form of payment.

12. **Look at the back of your company's checkbook periodically** to ensure that no checks are missing.

13. **Do not accept checks that have been "signed" with a rubber stamp** unless the person tendering the check is someone you do business with on a regular basis and know to be trustworthy. Even then, it's a good idea to have the check signed again in front of you.

 ## IF YOU ARE VICTIMIZED

As in most other white-collar crimes, the likelihood that a business will recoup money lost in a check fraud scheme depends on the actions taken as soon as the scheme is detected. Precaution is always your best defense—and in the case of check fraud, it often is your only defense. Even given state and federal laws, once a bad check has been passed, it is at best very difficult to recoup lost revenues.

Insufficient Funds

Most state laws allow those who pass checks on accounts with insufficient funds a week or two to make good. Even in states where this is not the law, many businesses allow the same leeway as part of a "good neighbor" policy.

If you have accepted a check written against insufficient funds, send the individual or business that issued the bad check a notice by registered mail. The notice should contain a copy (not the original) of the bad check along with a notice like the one printed on page 124, detailing your state's law or penal code against the passage of bad checks.

If the notice brings no response, follow-up phone calls or personal visits to the customer's home may prove more effective. Failing that, your next step might involve one of the following four options.

1. Ask your bank to put the check on "collection" status. Your bank will return the bad check to the issuer's bank, and when sufficient funds are collected in the issuer's account, the check will receive priority payment.

2. If this attempt proves unsuccessful, you can contact your local

NOTICE OF RETURNED CHECK

Dear Customer:

You will find outlined below information relating to your check recently returned to us unhonored. We realize the complexity of keeping accurate bank balances and know that you would like to honor your check. We appreciate your business and are sorry for the inconvenience.

10 day **NOTICE**	**RETURNED CHECK INFORMATION**	**10 day** **NOTICE**

You are hereby notified that your check dated _____ 19___, for $_____ has been presented to the bank for payment and has been returned to us unpaid. Please arrange to pay the amount of this check within ten (10) business days from the date you first receive this notice.

Date_____ _____(Store)
Signed_____ _____(Address)
Phone_____ _____(Town, State)

(PLACE CHECK HERE WHEN COPYING)

**[Quote your state's law or penal code
against the passage of bad checks]**

IMPORTANT—Please make your check good within 10 days! **If you fail to honor your check within 10 days after receiving this notice we will be forced to consider appropriate legal action.**

police department and protest the check. You will be asked to complete certain forms which then must be approved by the issuer's bank, and the police will issue a warrant for the issuer's arrest.

3. If the police determine that the size of the check does not merit their pursuit of the case, your company's attorney can file a civil complaint. A subpoena will be issued and a court date set.

4. As a last resort, you can turn the matter over to a collection agency. However, the rates charged by collection agencies usually are based on a large percentage of the amount they collect.

When You Suspect a Fraud

If you believe an individual is attempting to pass a bad check in your store or business:

- Attempt to stall the suspect without arousing suspicion.
- Call the police immediately.
- When the police arrive, let them interrogate the suspect, and follow their instructions.
- If the suspect flees before the police arrive, try to get a description of the suspect and any companions, the license number and a physical description of the car or other vehicle used, and the direction taken.

In Cases of Fraud

1. When your bank notifies you that a customer's check is fraudulent, immediately contact your local police department. Some retail establishments also may want to notify the retail division of their local Chamber of Commerce and their central security office to alert other stores in the area and branches of their own store.

2. Keep evidence in a safe, secure place. Place the check in a sealed envelope without folding, stapling, or marking it, and handle it as little as possible.

3. Be willing to prosecute. Authorities say that businesses that routinely prosecute bad-check passers reduce the likelihood of being victimized in the future. Professional criminals generally look for establishments that are "soft" on bad-check passers.

4. The passing of a bad out-of-state check is a federal offense. If you find you have accepted such a check, immediately contact your local branch of the FBI, listed in your telephone directory.

CHAPTER 12

THE CASE OF

The Free Lunch

Every day a number of different discount coupons are presented by customers at a fast-food restaurant and are redeemed for food. When coupons clipped from locally distributed coupon books begin appearing, the store manager redeems them and stacks them with the others. At the end of the month, the dollar value of all the coupons is tabulated, and they are mailed to the restaurant chain's headquarters for credit.

A week later the store manager receives a telephone call from headquarters. The coupons clipped from the locally distributed books were not authorized by the company and appear to be counterfeit. Even the "guaranteed redemption" offer printed on the back of the coupons has been falsified. Contacting local law enforcement officials, the store owner learns that his was only one of a number of

Coupon Fraud

area businesses that accepted counterfeit coupons. Fast-talking con artists apparently printed fictitious coupon books offering discounts at several hundred area businesses, and then sold the books in bulk and at a discount to area religious and social groups. Those unwitting accomplices handled the marketing and sales.

And, of course, by the time the coupons began appearing at area retailers and the scheme was uncovered, the culprits had long since left town.

A $2.5 Billion Business

To the average consumer, couponing represents a means of shaving a few dollars off the weekly grocery bill or enjoying an evening out at a reduced price. To retailers, couponing offers a way to revive business during a slow period or attract new customers. To companies manufacturing a product or providing a service, couponing is a time-tested method for introducing new products or services, or spurring sales. In any case, couponing today represents a $2.5-billion-a-year business that is growing daily.

When most consumers hear the word couponing, they think of those 5¢, 10¢, and 25¢ discount coupons that appear in newspa-

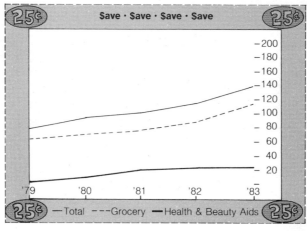

COUPONING TRENDS

Coupons Distributed 1979–83

(in billions)

Source: A. C. Nielson Co.

pers, magazines, and direct-mail packets. But in the 1980s, couponing has expanded dramatically. It is no longer unusual to receive coupons worth $50 or $100 off the purchase of a major appliance, or even several hundred dollars off the purchase of a new car.

Because coupons are redeemable for money, large blocks of misredeemed (credited against purchases which never occur) or counterfeit coupons can cost an advertiser or retailer thousands of dollars each month. And when coupons fall into the wrong hands, they don't stimulate the sale of products or services as intended. Thus, the damage is doubly expensive.

According to industry representatives, the hardest-hit victims of coupon fraud activities are product manufacturers. In most cases, it is the manufacturer who ends up paying for fraudulently redeemed coupons. However, with greater numbers of local merchants distributing their own coupons, swindlers increasingly are targeting these smaller, more susceptible merchants.

How Couponing Works

In its most basic form, a coupon is a written offer of a discounted or free product or service. A legitimate coupon will contain the terms of the offer and inform retailers that the issuer of the coupon will reimburse them for its face value.

Coupons are normally issued to prospective customers by the manufacturer of a product or provider of a service. The coupon may be redeemed, or bought back, from the consumer by the retailer selling that product or service. The majority of coupons are then sent by the retailer to a clearinghouse, rather than directly to the manufacturer or service provider. The clearinghouse sorts the different coupons, counts them, and tabulates their value. It then reimburses the retailer for the total value of coupons received. The clearinghouse ships the canceled coupons to the various manufacturers, which in turn pay the clearinghouse the face value of the coupons plus a handling charge for its services.

Because the redemption process involves so many different participating groups, there are numerous opportunities for coupon fraud. Among the most common abuses are:

- The sale of newspaper coupon inserts by newspaper employees

- The interception and sale of direct-mail coupons by postal workers

- The redemption by retailers of coupons for purchases of merchandise other than that specified by the manufacturers, and the subsequent submission of those coupons to the manufacturers for reimbursement

- The submission of illegally obtained coupons by clearinghouses to manufacturers

- The production of counterfeit coupons and their submission singly to local retailers or in bulk to clearinghouses

PROTECT YOUR BUSINESS

Couponing experts urge businesses that use coupons in their promotions to learn as much as possible about the persons or businesses that will be involved in distributing their coupons. Among the questions that should be addressed are:

- How are coupons or preprinted advertising inserts stored?

- Is there a security system to guard coupons or inserts against theft?

- What is the distribution process?

- How is theft by those distributing the coupons or inserts prevented?

- Are coupons or inserts that have not been distributed returned to the printer or advertiser? And, if so, what security precautions are taken?

- What is done with undistributed coupons or inserts that are not returned? Are they destroyed? And, if so, under what guidelines and security procedures?

With these questions in mind, be alert for distributors who show indications of:

- Little or no apparent security in the storage of coupons or inserts

- A poorly supervised or undocumented distribution and/or mailing system

- Lack of a clear-cut procedure for recovering or accounting for undistributed coupons or inserts

- No periodic checking system to determine whether coupons or inserts are distributed and disposed of properly

While it may be difficult for the average businessperson to detect or prevent coupon fraud, the first line of defense is an informed skepticism. If you are approached by someone offering a dubious plan, don't become involved until you are certain that it is a legitimate business arrangement. For example, don't let anyone persuade you that it is a regular course of business to sell coupons in bulk to another person or business at a discounted price—the only transfers of money in couponing should take place between the consumer and the retailer, and between the retailer and the advertiser or its clearinghouse.

Also remember that your business is not required to accept coupons that you suspect are counterfeit. Counterfeit coupons usually are poorly printed copies of the originals, with the printing in one color and on one side only. Legitimate coupons should give the name and address of the manufacturer, an expiration date or indication that there is none, and a description of redemption guidelines. Businesses that use coupons in their promotions can make the counterfeiter's job more difficult by issuing coupons that contain all these elements and are printed on both sides and in at least two colors.

Newspaper Industry Guidelines

The Audit Bureau of Circulations, an organization of advertisers, advertising agencies, and newspaper and periodical publishers, recommends that businesses using newspapers for coupon or insert distribution insist on the newspapers' compliance with the following industry guidelines.

1. When inserts are provided by the business, the paper should verify that:

   - The number of inserts received matches the number shipped

   - Inserts are placed in a secure area until removed by authorized personnel

   - Inserts are placed in the newspaper for distribution according to the agreement

   - Leftover inserts are disposed of in a manner that makes them unusable for redemption

2. When the newspaper prints the inserts, its circulation department should verify that:

- Press room reports or statements list the number of sections run for each issue

- Spoiled coupon sections and sections leftover after printing and insertion are disposed of in a manner that makes them unusable for redemption

- Coupon sections printed prior to the date of insertion are placed in a secure area until removed by authorized personnel for insertion in the newspaper

- Printing plates or other material used to print coupon sections are disposed of properly

3. When the coupon or insert distribution is completed, you should ask the newspaper's circulation department for:

- Auditable records or statements to confirm the disposition of returns, leftovers, and unsold copies from employees, distributors, carriers, drivers, and others responsible for the recovery and destruction of newspapers containing advertiser coupons

- Statements from waste-paper companies or other firms that purchase newspaper copies containing advertising coupons that coupons are disposed of in a manner that makes them unusable for redemption

 IF YOU ARE VICTIMIZED

If you have been the victim of coupon fraud, a number of federal and state laws may have been violated. If the fraud involves the counterfeit reproduction of coupons, federal laws involving counterfeiting and trademark and copyright laws may have bearing. If the fraud involves transactions by the U.S. mail, a number of postal fraud laws may come into play.

The first step a manufacturer or other coupon issuer should take when fraud has occurred is to stop payment on any questionable coupon redemptions. If the alleged fraud involves possible misredemption on the part of another business or franchise, the manufacturer should demand proof of purchase.

If the U.S. mail has been involved, contact local U.S. postal authorities or the Chief Postal Inspector, U.S. Postal Service (See

Appendix A), and ask for an investigation of potential coupon fraud. The postal service will in turn contact your local U.S. Attorney General's office and ask for an indictment, if warranted. You should also contact the U.S. Attorney General's office, listed in your telephone directory.

In addition, report the fraud to your local Better Business Bureau (See Appendix B). The BBB will include the information in its files to alert future inquirers.

CHAPTER 13

THE CASE OF

The Wheeler-Dealers

A major food wholesaler services hundreds of grocery stores in a tri-state area. Thousands of cartons of boxed and canned food are delivered every week by the wholesaler's fleet of tractor-trailer trucks, and because of the large volume of shipments, a certain percentage of losses through ruptured cartons, broken glass containers, and otherwise damaged or misplaced merchandise is built into costs.

When the accounting department decides to take a close look at these losses, it discovers that the large majority can be attributed to three of the drivers. Contacting the managers of the groceries serviced by those drivers, accounting further discovers that, for a number of the stores, short deliveries are a small but recurring problem. The wholesaler hires a private detective firm to discreetly investigate the problem.

Cargo Theft

Several weeks of observation and inquiry reveal that the three inventive drivers have come up with a simple plan for supplementing their income. By short-shipping their regular customers, they are able to make deliveries to several small, private groceries that pay for the cartons of food in cash. The drivers pocket the money and report to their employer that the missing cartons were damaged and discarded in transit, or that their trucks were shorted at the loading dock.

The dishonest drivers are turned over to the police. The lost revenues, which over a three-year period have amounted to more than $100,000, are never recovered.

Multidollar "Roll"

Between $1 billion and $3 billion are lost annually through cargo theft, according to the U.S. Department of Transportation. Most cargo theft occurs in freight handling areas. The thieves may be customers working in collusion with shipping company employees, highway bandits who rob delivery vehicles in transit, department workers employed by the shipping company or by an independent shipper hired to handle distribution, or truck drivers or others involved in the delivery process. But most often they are employees. According to American Trucking Associations estimates, as much as 70 percent of all cargo theft losses may be attributed to employee dishonesty.

CARGO LOSSES BY CAUSE OF LOSS

Claims Paid By National Freight Claim Council of American Trucking Associations in 1982

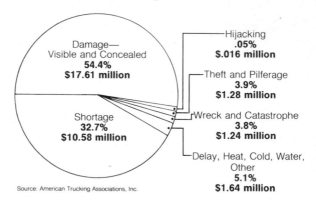

Damage—
Visible and Concealed
54.4%
$17.61 million

Hijacking
.05%
$.016 million

Theft and Pilferage
3.9%
$1.28 million

Shortage
32.7%
$10.58 million

Wreck and Catastrophe
3.8%
$1.24 million

Delay, Heat, Cold, Water,
Other
5.1%
$1.64 million

Source: American Trucking Associations, Inc.

PROTECT YOUR BUSINESS

Given the high level of employee complicity, the keystone of any security program is careful pre-employment screening. A thorough pre-employment check includes examining the backgrounds of prospects with an eye to work experience, arrests and convictions, and credit history.

A chronological look at the steps involved in the shipment of cargo points out the areas of opportunity for crime—and the steps businesses can take at each stage to thwart the criminals.

1. **The shipping process begins when an authorized employee or manager fills out or signs orders approving the shipment of merchandise to another company.**

   An unauthorized shipment begins in the same way, but in this case, no legitimate order has been placed and the merchandise may be shipped to a drop-off point selected by the employee. The evidence of illegal activity is camouflaged by either destroying or altering invoices or shipping instructions. In a fraudulent *overshipment*, excess goods are shipped and subsequently sold by an accomplice at the receiving end.

   Problems are more prevalent in companies that do not investigate or require the return of overshipped merchandise. A strictly controlled ordering and invoicing system is an important first step in reducing the risk of unauthorized shipments. Ideally, all sales tickets should be numbered, and these numbers and the sales they represent logged at least once a week in a sales register. Spoiled, mismarked, or canceled sales tickets should be clearly marked "VOID" and turned over to an authorized billing clerk.

   Some businesses find the use of a sales receipt register helpful in encouraging salespeople to keep careful and complete records. These machines "crank out" prenumbered sales tickets and automatically "crank forward" copies of completed sales tickets into a sealed compartment, access to which should be limited to an authorized billing clerk.

   Customer invoices should be handled in a similar controlled, numbered fashion, and sealed invoice registers, with access to the secured copies limited to authorized accounting personnel, may be a valuable precaution.

   If possible, products also should be numbered, either individually or in crates, and the numbers corresponding to the products recorded on the sales ticket, shipping instructions, and invoice. These numbers can then be checked against inventory records by the auditing or accounting department.

2. **The merchandise is assembled and packaged for transit—commonly called the staging process.**

   Theft at this stage of shipment is often made possible by disorganization. The most crime-ridden assembly areas are those in which employee and customer access are not controlled, products are not arranged in an organized manner, and sound inventory control procedures are not followed. Dishonest employees and customers may take advantage of the lack of order by walking off with merchandise or concealing it for later removal.

137

Careful planning and organization can virtually eliminate theft during the staging process. The assembly and packaging of goods for shipment should always take place in an area specifically set aside for that purpose, such as a warehouse or packaging plant—*never* at a loading dock or similar area where merchandise is readily visible and accessible to employees and customers. Access to the staging area should be limited to assigned employees and should be watched over by a manager or security guard. Inventory control should be required at every stage of the process. A sound inventory control system might operate in the following manner.

- *Sales tickets* are handed to an employee solely responsible for pulling the merchandise from stock. That employee writes the product registration or inventory number on the sales ticket. Some warehouses attach a removable inventory control number to every item, which is removed from the carton and attached to the sales ticket. When the order has been

CARGO THEFT AND PILFERAGE

Claims Paid By National Freight Claim Council in 198 [By Commodity]

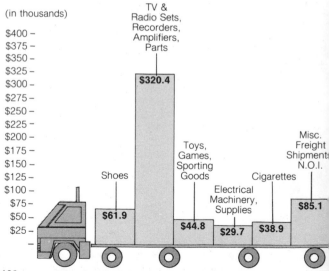

(in thousands)

Source: National Freight Claim Council of American Trucking Associations, Inc.

filled, the employee initials the sales ticket and passes it on to

- *a second employee* who is responsible for checking the merchandise against the sales ticket, initialing the sales ticket, and packaging the merchandise. That employee then passes on the sales ticket to

- *the accounting department,* which records the inventory control numbers in an inventory register.

Employees involved in the assembly and packaging process should be regularly rotated from their assignments. A member of management should periodically oversee the staging procedure to ensure its proper execution and should examine shipments at random to verify that orders are being filled properly.

3. **Merchandise is loaded onto trucks for transit.**

The loading process can provide dishonest employees and customers with fertile opportunities for theft. In poorly controlled

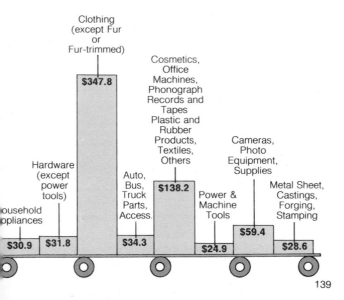

operations where customers and employees are permitted to congregate in the loading area, cargo can easily be carried off and concealed in waiting trucks or cars. *Short packaging* is another common loading dock crime. Employees divert a truck driver's attention long enough to slip packages away from the driver's shipment, and the driver then signs the delivery receipt, acknowledging that he has verified the count of the shipment. Usually the driver does not realize he has been shortchanged until after his delivery. At that stage, he is held responsible for the shortage.

Precautions similar to those used to limit access and control activities in the staging area also can be effective in preventing theft in the cargo area.

- Limit access to authorized personnel and vehicles.

- One employee should be made responsible for overseeing each transaction or shipment. That employee should initial the delivery receipt, thereby verifying that the proper merchandise has left the loading dock.

- If possible, one employee should handle the physical transfer of the merchandise, and another, preferably a member of management, should oversee the accuracy of the transaction.

- Employees should be periodically rotated in their assignments. The drivers, or whoever picks up the merchandise, should be required to examine the shipment and sign the delivery receipt.

4. **The merchandise is transported by truck or tractor-trailer to the point of delivery.**

   Theft directly from delivery vehicles may involve the pilferage of small, costly items from a shipment, commonly called tailgate theft, or robbery by force of the entire contents of a truck.

   Before the shipment leaves the store or warehouse, its contents should be listed on a roster, with copies provided to the company selling the merchandise, the delivery company (if different), the receiving company, and the driver. When the contents are loaded and in transit, observe the following precautions.

- Keep merchandise under lock and key at all times.

- Where theft is likely, avoid the use of flatbed trucks that make merchandise visible and accessible.

- Loaded vehicles that are parked overnight should be locked so that the delivery doors cannot be opened; for example, back to back.

- The parking area should be well-lit, and, where possible, guarded. Some large truck stops provide protected areas for a reasonable fee.
- Avoid parking loaded delivery vehicles in high-risk areas, such as inner cities.
- Alarms should be installed in delivery vehicles, particularly those that often must be parked overnight when full of merchandise.
- Schedules should be arranged so that, whenever possible, shipments can be made without overnight stops.
- When a shipment requires the use of more than one vehicle or when several vehicles are heading in the same direction, they should travel together in a convoy.
- A security guard in a separate vehicle should follow shipments of particularly high value or risk.
- Information on shipment contents, departure and arrival times, and route plans should be kept confidential.
- Radio or telephone communication devices should be installed in all delivery vehicles.
- Mark the company's name and address on all sides of delivery vehicles so that police can quickly identify stolen vehicles.

 IF YOU ARE VICTIMIZED

Cargo theft should be handled like any other form of theft. If you observe an employee or customer in the process of committing the crime, contact your local police department immediately. Try to detain the suspect as long as possible *without using force*, and, if possible, without arousing suspicion. If the suspect leaves the premises before the police arrive, have ready a detailed description of the suspect and any companions, and, if possible, the license number and description of the suspect's car or other vehicle. Also try to make note of the direction the suspect takes when leaving. Any further investigation should be left to the police.

If cargo theft occurs in transit, immediately contact local police authorities. State police should also be provided with a detailed description of stolen merchandise and, if possible, of the suspects and get-away vehicle.

When the police determine that the interstate transfer of stolen goods is involved, the FBI also should be notified.

SECTION III

INTERNAL
CRIME

CHAPTER 14

THE CASE OF

The Cooked Books

The controller for a small retail operation seemed an exemplary, practically indispensable, employee. The woman had started in accounts receivable when the store first opened, and ten years later she was solely responsible for handling billing, accounts receivable, audits, and customer complaints. Rarely taking a day off and never a full week's vacation, she impressed fellow workers and company owners with her hard work and dedication.

The controller reaped the rewards of her labors. She owned an impressive home, a weekend cottage, and new cars every other year. No one had ever questioned her ability to afford these niceties—until the time she became ill and was hospitalized, and the owners were forced to take over her financial responsibilities.

Several customer complaints about inaccurate billings raised troubling questions and prompted a careful examination of the records—an examination that gradually uncovered the elements of a

Pilferage
and
Embezzlement

meticulously planned scheme that for years had been allowing the controller to secretly embezzle thousands of dollars from company profits. A key facet of her scheme involved the regular pocketing of all or a portion of cash payments on open accounts and the altering of company records and subsequent invoices to acknowledge receipt of lesser sums. Because she was in charge of all aspects of the company's billing and recordkeeping, the controller could successfully accomplish and camouflage this and other deceptions.

While the woman was eventually fired and found guilty of embezzlement, the company would never completely recuperate from the loss of revenues.

Crimes of Confidence

In 1984, the National Institute of Justice, research branch of the U.S. Department of Justice, estimated that in the early 1980s, losses to business from pilferage and embezzlement amounted to between $10 billion and $20 billion annually. Losses actually may be significantly higher than estimated, says the Institute, because many of these crimes go either undetected or unreported.

One-third of all office and plant workers steal from employers while on the job, estimates the Institute. And according to the U.S. Chamber of Commerce, from five to eight percent of employees steal regularly and "in volume," and from 60 to 75 percent of all shortages may be attributed to employee theft.

Pilferage and embezzlement are the most common types of employee theft, with pilferage the more prevalent of the two. While both crimes involve deception by employees, they differ in the level of trust accorded employees by their employers.

PERCENT OF RETAIL EMPLOYEE INVOLVEMENT IN PROPERTY THEFT

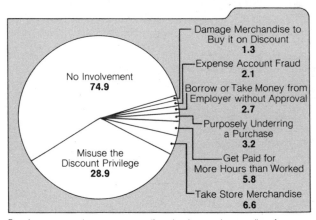

Based on responses to anonymous questionnaires by a random sampling of 3,567 retail store employees

Source: *Theft by Employees in Work Organizations*, published by the National Institute of Justice, 1983

PILFERAGE

The theft of a company's goods and commodities by its employees, or pilferage, does not require the altering of a company's financial records, and is usually carried out by employees who have access to merchandise but little or no access to company records or bookkeeping.

Among the many techniques used by pilfering employees are: concealing merchandise inside clothing or packages; using products directly from a retail store's shelves; hiding merchandise in trash receptacles for pick-up at a later time; purposely breaking or damaging products, reporting the damage, and taking the "worthless" merchandise home; conspiring with delivery people or employees of a company doing business with one's employer to remove merchandise from the premises; replacing a container full of merchandise with an empty or partially full container; and running personal mail through the company postage meter.

 ## PROTECT YOUR BUSINESS

Most pilferers are otherwise honest individuals who probably don't think of themselves as thieves. Strategically posted diplomatic reminders reminding employees that pilferage erodes the funds that otherwise could go into wages, benefits, and company growth can help reduce the incidence of pilferage by such individuals. Other preventative measures should aim at removing both temptation and opportunity. A clear-cut policy that outlines acceptable working procedures and details the company's approach to pilferage might include some of the following guidelines. All these steps are not appropriate for all businesses, but where they can be observed, they should prove effective deterrents.

- **All employees should be required** to enter and leave the workplace through a designated employee entrance that is watched over by a security guard or management personnel. A coatroom should be provided for overcoats and unusually large packages. A sign posted at this entrance warning employees that "pilferage is a crime and those caught will be prosecuted" may be an effective deterrent.

- **Access to supply areas** should be restricted and watched over by a security guard or kept under lock and key. Employees who enter the supply area should be accompanied by a warehouse employee. A sign-in sheet should be filled out with names, times of entrance and departure, and merchandise removed.

- **Stockroom merchandise** should be kept in neat stacks, rather than disorderly piles, so that it is easy to spot when items are missing.

- **Employees should be restricted** in the use of photocopying machines, company gas pumps, telephones, postage meters, and other facilities designated "for company use only."

- **Guests, employees of other companies,** and others who are not direct employees of the company always should be escorted to their appointments by an employee.

- **Employees of one department** should be rotated to a different department for taking inventory, or inventory taking should be supervised by a member of management.

- **Merchandise should be kept** in neat, orderly displays and should never be stacked near openable windows or doors.

- **Company equipment** should be clearly marked with the company's name, and tools should be inventoried and locked up by a supervisor at the end of each workday.

- **Be suspicious** of company equipment or merchandise that appears to be out of place. Encourage employees to report out-of-place items to management.

- **Shipping and receiving activities** should be based in separate areas of a company's facilities. Only merchandise authorized for shipments should be permitted in the shipping area, and a security guard should be posted to ensure that no merchandise leaves the premises through the receiving area.

- **Security or management personnel** periodically should inspect or sift through rubbish piles or garbage containers for concealed items.

- **Product components** used on assembly lines should be inventoried and kept in secure areas. Only the amount of material required for each day's production should be removed from the secured area.

- **Employees should be assured** that the identity of anyone who reports dishonesty on the part of other employees will be held in confidence. Telephone hotlines can be installed or offers of rewards for such information posted, but management should be aware that many honest employees may be unwilling to "snitch" on fellow workers and that the system can be misused by a vindictive employee who turns in another to satisfy a personal grudge.

EMBEZZLEMENT

The embezzler's crime involves the fraudulent appropriation or conversion to personal use or benefit of company money or property. Culprits commonly are highly trusted employees who have access to a company's records, cash, and/or merchandise. Their crimes range from simple cash register thefts of small amounts of money to elaborate, long-term schemes involving the juggling of company books to conceal the theft of thousands, even millions of dollars in cash or merchandise.

The Small Business Administration reports that in the cases it has investigated, embezzlers generally have been given more authority than was necessary in their positions.

The methods used by embezzlers are limited only by the imagination. The most common schemes—non-registered sales, lapping, check-kiting, payroll fraud, the creation of dummy suppliers, and expense account fraud—are briefly described below.

Non-registered sales occur when a cashier purposely fails to ring a sale in the cash register and steals the cash that should have been deposited for the sale. Most non-registered sales are made possible by situations in which a customer pressed for time leaves the store without a receipt. The cashier may then ring an amount less than that received or make a "no sale" ring. Most cashiers who commit this crime keep secret records of the amount they have accumulated in the drawer so they can remove the correct amount of cash when the opportunity arises.

Lapping involves the temporary withholding of funds, such as payments on accounts receivable. This form of embezzlement is an ongoing scheme that usually starts with the theft of a small amount of cash but can run into thousands of dollars. For example, an employee responsible for recording payments to a company pockets a $50 cash payment. He then covers the theft by applying part of a separate, larger payment to the $50 invoice. The employee continues to skim funds from the payments to cover previous short payments and pockets increasingly large sums as the scheme expands.

The lapping scheme requires the dishonest employee to keep close track of the various shortages and transfers to avoid drawing attention to a short account. The embezzler usually has access to accounts receivable records and can continually alter statements to customers, so that this type of fraud may continue undetected for years.

Check-kiting can be accomplished only by an employee who is in a position to write checks and make deposits in two or more bank accounts. One of these accounts will be a company account; the other is usually an account opened by the employee in his or her own name. Less often, both will be company accounts in different banks. And in yet another scenario, the second account will be with another company where an accomplice of the embezzler is working the same scheme on his employer.

The dishonest check writer takes advantage of the "float," or the period between when a company deposits a check and the bank collects the funds.

Floating a Kite

Assuming a three-day "float," an embezzler can carry out the following check-kiting scheme.

On day one a check for $5,000 drawn on Bank A is deposited in Bank B. The next day the check-kiter cashes a check for $5,000, drawn on Bank B, with a teller at Bank B. Since the original kited check will be presented to Bank A for collection of funds on day four, the check-kiter will deposit a check on or before that date in Bank A for $6,000 drawn on Bank B. This both ensures payment of the original kited check and increases the amount of the kite. As the process is repeated, the amounts of the kited checks become larger, more cash is withdrawn, and the scheme can continue until the shortage is uncovered—or until the kite "breaks" when one of the banks refuses to honor a kited check because the funds on deposit are uncollected.

Payroll frauds occur when a dishonest employee, usually one involved in payroll activities or a member of management with the authority to hire, adds the names of relatives or fictitious individuals to the company payroll. Payroll checks issued to those individuals are then either cashed by the relative and split with the employee, or cashed by the employee under a falsified signature.

Dummy suppliers may be created by an employee who has the authority to conduct purchases on behalf of the company. The employee falsifies documentation to authorize a nonexistent purchase, "bills" the company for the purchase, and subsequently pays the fictitious invoice. In some cases, large corporations have made out monthly payments of thousands of dollars for purchases that were never actually made to companies that existed in name only.

Expense account fraud is one of the easiest and most common ways employees embezzle funds. Personal items may be bought and charged to the company; receipts may be falsified to document expense account claims; expenses may be charged to the company for "entertaining" individuals who could not legitimately be considered current or potential customers. In a related offense, employees with liberal telephone accounts may charge to their employer numerous personal long-distance calls.

Read the Signs

Embezzlers may tip their hands to the alert businessperson through some of these tell-tale signs.

- Accounting, inventory, and other company books that are not kept up to date
- Customer invoices that habitually are mailed late
- Frequent complaints by customers that statements are inaccurate
- Employees who regularly turn down promotions or refuse vacations
- Employees who frequently ask for cash advances on paychecks
- Employees who frequently are entertained by suppliers, or who submit expense accounts that include costly entertainment charges
- Employees whose standards of living are much higher than seems possible on their income
- Frequent inventory shortages
- Slow collections, which may indicate that payments are being sidetracked on their way to the company's bank account
- Unusual bad-debt write-offs by the accounting department

PROTECT YOUR BUSINESS

The Small Business Administration (SBA) indicates that one of the most important steps the owner or manager of a business can take to prevent embezzlement is to set a positive and clear-cut example of the proper manner of conducting business. Employers who dip into petty cash, fudge on expense accounts, or use company funds or equipment for personal activities may unwittingly encourage employees to follow their lead.

An employer should establish and maintain a working climate of accountability in which accurate records are kept and regularly audited. The SBA also recommends the following procedures.

- **Carefully check** the background of prospective employees, particularly those to be given fiduciary responsibilities. This check should include oral and written contacts with previous employers, credit bureaus, and personal references. Make sure that an employee who will handle funds is adequately bonded.

- **An owner or member of senior management** should supervise the accounting employee who opens and records receipts of checks, cash payments, and money orders.

- **Bank deposits** should be prepared daily and made by an owner or manager. Duplicate deposit slips, stamped ''received'' by the bank, should always be returned to the accounting department.

- **All payments** should be approved by senior management as well as by the person who draws or signs the checks.

- **Senior management** should examine all invoices and supporting data before signing checks. Management should verify that merchandise was received and that prices seem reasonable. In many false purchase schemes, the embezzler will neglect to make up receiving forms or other records purporting to show receipt of merchandise.

- **All paid invoices** should be marked ''canceled'' and filed in a secure area to prevent double payment. Dishonest accounting department employees have been known to make out and receive approval on duplicate checks for the same invoice. The second check may be embezzled by the employee or by an accomplice at the company issuing the invoice.

- **Prenumbered checkbooks** and other prenumbered forms should be periodically inspected to ensure that checks or forms from the back or middle of the books have not been removed for use in a fraudulent scheme.

- **Employees responsible** for making sales or assigning projects to outside suppliers should not be permitted to process transactions affecting their own accounts.

- **The reconciliation** of bank statements and canceled checks should be done by an employee who does not draw or sign checks. Management should examine canceled checks, and endorsements for unusual features (See Chapter 11, Check Fraud).

- **Payroll should be prepared** by one person, checked by another, and distributed by others not involved with payroll preparation or timeslip approvals.

- **Names placed on payroll** should be authorized in writing by a specifically designated company official.

- **Shipments should be authorized** and accounted for by an employee who is not also responsible for controlling inventories. An employee who maintains inventory records should not participate in physical counts of inventory or in reconciliation of physical counts with the records.

- **Where non-registered sales** are suspected, retail establishments may effectively enlist the customer's assistance. Signs posted by each cash register announcing that any customer who does not receive a sales receipt with every purchase is entitled to a cash bonus may help to put an end to the problem. Also effective are outside "shoppers," who may be hired through private shopping services and, sometimes, local women's clubs or auxiliaries. Shoppers are provided with funds to make purchases in the store, and they can provide valuable information on whether sales are being recorded properly, and on the proficiency and courtesy of salespeople.

- **A responsible company official** who is not on the accounting department's staff should be designated to receive and investigate customer complaints.

 IF YOU ARE VICTIMIZED

If you believe your company has been the victim of an embezzlement scheme, *do not confront the suspect*. All too often, situations that seem to indicate impropriety on the part of an employee turn out to have perfectly valid explanations. The SBA reports cases in which employees have been charged with embezzlement, dismissed from their positions, and later found to be entirely innocent. A false accusation could involve your company in a lawsuit.

If you suspect foul play, contact a trustworthy independent accountant who can thoroughly examine company books with an eye for possible embezzlement activities. If, with the guidance of your accountant, you still believe that one or more employees may be guilty of embezzlement, contact your attorney for advice on how to proceed. Discuss with your attorney the necessity of notifying the bonding company and appropriate law enforcement authorities. It is particularly important that you follow legal advice in matters regarding prosecution so that your company will not be subject to charges of false arrest.

CHAPTER 15

The Collusive Consultant

The head of research at one major corporation is responsible for "farming out" special projects to qualified consultants and subcontractors. A subcontractor bidding on a large project invites her to discuss business over lunch. The research head mentions that money has been tight and raises small at her company in recent years. She is hoping to supplement her income by doing some outside consulting. Independent consultants are often used by his firm, says the subcontractor. If he is awarded this particular job, his firm could probably use the services of someone with her professional expertise.

At subsequent meetings the research head and subcontractor become more at ease in discussing the arrangement. They agree on

Bribery, Kickbacks, and Payoffs

a "mutually beneficial" plan—she will provide outside professional advice for a monthly fee of $1,000; the silent arrangement will run the length of the contract.

The subcontractor is recommended for the project and approved. Work runs several months longer than expected but is completed satisfactorily, according to the report submitted by the research head to her superiors. Subsequent projects are bid on and awarded to the same subcontractor.

Over the following ten years, the research head receives more than $100,000 in "consultant fees" from the subcontractor. These fees are passed along in the subcontractor's bills—which are approved by the head of research.

Behind the Schemes

Arrangements such as the one described above involve employees and public and private officials at virtually every level of government, industry, business, and labor. A 1975 study by the American Management Association concluded that commercial bribery, kickbacks, and payoffs cost U.S. businesses at least $3.5 billion and possibly as much as $10 billion annually. By 1990, the Association estimates, that figure may be doubled.

The motivating factors behind bribery, kickback, and payoff schemes are innumerable. Most common among the goals of perpetrators are attempts to:

- Obtain new business or retain old business
- Solicit approval on plans or permits from government officials
- Influence local, state, or federal legislation
- Obtain government licenses
- Obtain approval on loans
- Prevent work stoppages due to actions of union officials
- Obtain proprietary information
- Obtain approvals on falsified financial statements
- Encourage the sale of stocks or bonds at distorted prices
- Obtain information on bids submitted by contractors
- Facilitate the sale of inferior products or services
- Sway the minds of law enforcement officials
- Pay off gambling or other personal debts
- Cover up the lavish use of entertainment or other company funds

Enlightening Inquiries

While variations on these schemes run into the thousands, the majority can be grouped into two categories: schemes involving dealings between business and government, and schemes involving dealings among private-sector parties.

Research by the federal government's National Advisory Commission on Criminal Justice Standards and Goals as well as the U.S. Chamber of Commerce led to the development of a series of questions that should be asked when bribery, kickbacks, or payoff schemes are suspected. Affirmative answers to any of the following questions do not necessarily indicate fraudulent activity but should be regarded as signs that something could be awry.

In Government/Business Dealings

1. Do respected and well-qualified companies refuse to conduct business with the city, state, or federal agency?

2. Are government contracts awarded to a small number of firms?

3. Is competitive bidding not required?

4. Are there frequent "emergency" situations that do not require competitive bidding?

5. Are professional services bid "by invitation only"?

6. Have low bids been disclosed, and the low-bidding companies subsequently disqualified for unspecified technical reasons?

7. Do businesses encounter significant delays when applying for county, local, state, or federal licenses, such as liquor licenses and building permits?

8. Are government procedures so complicated that a go-between is often required to unravel the mystery and get through to the right people?

9. Do government officials or employees have financial or other interests in businesses competing for government business?

10. Have public officials accepted high posts with companies to which their agencies have recently awarded contracts?

11. Are antibribery statutes ineffective, or limited in scope to cover department heads only?

12. Do large campaign contributions precede (or follow) favorable government rulings?

13. Are costs of conducting similar business operations, after allowances are made for legitimate differences in labor rates, transportation, and other factors, markedly different in two counties or states?

In Business-to-Business Dealings

1. Are reputable dealers uninterested in submitting bids?

2. Is there frequent use, without periodic bidding, of the same supplier?

3. Do certain employees pass up opportunities for promotion for questionable reasons?

4. Does an employee frequently socialize with a supplier?

5. Is the standard of living of anyone who influences company

157

purchases higher than can be explained by wage or salary levels or other legitimate sources of income?

6. Does the cost of certain goods or services seem inexplicably high?

7. Does one individual hold the sole responsibility for calling for, reviewing, and approving bids?

8. Are there vague "extra charges"?

9. Does an employee who influences the selection of suppliers have a financial interest in, or relatives employed by, current suppliers?

10. Does an employee who influences the selection of suppliers obtain tickets for sporting events, concerts, or other social galas with inexplicable ease?

 PROTECT YOUR BUSINESS

Both the National Advisory Commission on Criminal Justice Standards and Goals and the U.S. Chamber of Commerce recommend these measures to combat bribery, payoff, and kickback schemes.

In Government/Business Dealings

1. Management in both government and business should prohibit the exchanging of gifts, regardless of value.

2. Government and business should ban all activities that carry even the appearance of impropriety.

3. Local and state governments should appoint and maintain nonpolitical commissions to continually monitor and investigate possible official corruption.

4. Solicitations of payoffs by public officials should be reported to appropriate law enforcement agencies.

In Business-to-Business Dealings

1. Businesses should separate receiving from purchasing operations so buyers cannot accept short deliveries in return for kickbacks.

2. Businesses should require competitive bidding.

3. An executive from outside the purchasing department should review bids and inspect incoming goods.

4. Employees, particularly those in purchasing, should be required to file monthly reports on gifts and gratuities received. A limit should be set on the value of gifts that may be accepted.

5. Management should insist that gifts come to the office, not to employees' homes.

6. Vendors should be informed of acceptable gift-giving practices.

7. Businesses should insist that, in cases when a supplier other than the low bidder is selected, the reason be documented and sent to top management for review and approval.

8. Purchasing agents and suppliers should be rotated periodically.

9. Employees should be instructed to report any demands by customers for payoffs.

10. Estimates of reasonable costs for products and services should be developed so that possible kickback costs can be identified.

11. Policies should be developed that ensure maintenance of a professional distance between management and union officials.

12. Procedures should be instituted that alert management when payments of "commissions" are not documented by the usual paperwork, when "commissions" are not in line with recognized trade practices, and when payments are made through banks not usually used.

 # IF YOU ARE VICTIMIZED

An employee or official of a company or government organization involved in a bribery, kickback, or payoff scheme may have violated any of a number of local, state, or federal laws.

If you suspect that one of your employees is either receiving or giving bribes or kickbacks in dealings with another nongovernment firm, *do not confront the suspect* immediately. Instead, discuss your suspicions with your company attorneys to determine what action and investigation can be undertaken and what laws apply. It is essential that your business stay within the letter of the law; therefore, do not attempt an investigation on your own. And remember, it is not necessary that a bribe, kickback, or payoff actually be received in order for a crime to have been committed. Under most existing legislation, the mere offering, conferring, or agreeing to confer a benefit is considered an offense.

CHAPTER 16

THE CASE OF

The Crooked Claimant

A corporation provides automobiles for use by employees on company business, but occasionally a car is difficult to come by and employees are called upon to use their own vehicles. In these instances, the company provides mileage and usage reimbursement and accident coverage under a rider to its vehicle insurance policy.

One salesperson, who often goes directly from his home to client locations, reports early on a Monday morning that his car has been the victim of a hit-and-run accident. He is instructed to summon local police to the parking lot where the accident occurred. The police subsequently file an accident report and the company's insur-

Insurance Fraud

ance policy covers the repairs to the employee's car, less the $200 deductible, which is paid by the company.

What the company does not, and may never, know is that the car actually was damaged in a single-car accident over the weekend. Rather than contact his own insurance company and pay the deductible, plus risk the possibility of an increase in his insurance rates, the employee waited until Monday, drove to a client's office, and then reported the accident for filing at his employer's expense.

The Faces of Fraud

The American Insurance Association, representing more than 150 major insurance companies, estimates that anywhere from 10 to 25 percent of all claims filed may be fraudulent. The estimate's wide range, says an Association spokesperson, results from the number of possible interpretations of the term "insurance fraud," with the 10 percent figure limited to such highly fraudulent activities as auto theft rings and organized crime activities, and the 25 percent figure including even "small" frauds, such as claim figures submitted that are higher than actual costs.

While a 1974 estimate put total annual losses due to fraud at $1.5 billion, the American Insurance Association estimates that by 1982 the number had grown to $4 billion and was continuing its upward spiral. An Association spokesperson emphasizes that even this $4 billion figure is a conservative estimate, reflecting only "direct," accountable losses.

Other, nondirect losses due to insurance fraud include an average 15 percent increase built into insurance policy premiums to cover fraudulent claims. Unaccounted-for losses to business include the lost services of employees "recuperating" from fake accidents or illnesses, and unwarranted out-of-court settlements paid to insurance con artists by businesses wishing to avoid costly legal proceedings.

Because many businesspeople look upon insurance coverage as an unavoidable cost of doing business, they may not spend enough time examining how their policies work, what is and is not insured, and how insurance fraud can harm their business. Although a full treatment of the subject of insurance demands its own book, the most common types of insurance fraud are generally quite simple to understand. These schemes include:

- **the creation of fictitious insurance companies** that exist only in their paper policies

- **the sale of policies** by insurance companies that do not adhere to widely accepted business and insurance industry standards and as a result are more susceptible to failure and bankruptcy

- **the oversale of insurance,** resulting in coverage more extensive than is necessary

- **the fraudulent and deceitful activities** of customers and employees that result in unwarranted insurance claims

PROTECT YOUR BUSINESS

"Paper Firms"

To avoid doing business with a "paper" insurance company, your business should make a thorough investigation of the company being considered. Contact your local Better Business Bureau and the area office of your State Insurance Commissioner, listed in your telephone directory, for a report on the company. Request a copy of the firm's financial statement and have your accountant review the document to confirm that it has been certified by a reputable accounting firm and that the members of the company's board are reputable and serve in the company's best interest.

Do not hesitate to ask the insurance company for bank and business client references and to contact those references. Ask business clients for details of their associations with the insurance company—has it been responsive to their requests, made an effort to keep policies up to date, and kept them abreast of changes in the insurance industry that may affect their business?

Be particularly painstaking in your investigations when considering doing business with a foreign insurance firm.

Unsound Practices

To avoid doing business with an insurance company that fails to adhere to accepted industry standards, observe the precautions detailed above, paying particular attention to the State Insurance Commissioner's advice. Where little information is available about the financial stability of an insurance company, as may be the case with a firm located outside the U.S., ask a business investment counselor, such as a banker or broker, to assist in determining the insurer's stability and reliability. If doubts remain, look for another company.

Too Much Coverage?

There is a fine line between the proper amount of insurance coverage and too little or too much coverage. While it is important for a business to build a close working relationship with a reliable and responsive insurance broker, it also makes sense to occasionally have a competitive firm review your coverage with an eye to potential loopholes or excesses.

A colleague in a similar business, or a trade or business association to which you belong may be able to provide you with recommendations on business insurance coverage and the reliability of various insurers. Some associations offer group insurance packages as part of their member services; these packages may offer competitive rates and, because the insurer is familiar with the particular business, may have a better understanding of needs unique to the association's members.

Insurance Companies Fight Back

Insurance companies pay out billions of dollars each year in settlement for fraudulent claims that include staged accidents, phony burglaries, padded doctor's bills, falsified product liability claims, and one of the largest and most dangerous schemes, arson-for-profit. In 1980, fires of suspicious or incendiary origin—a major portion of which may be cases of arson-for-profit—were responsible for an estimated 770 deaths and $1.76 billion in damage, according to the National Fire Protection Association.

Insurance cheats come from all walks of life. Organized crime groups, terrorist organizations who stage accidents and file claims as a means of raising funds, unscrupulous professionals, including doctors, lawyers, and chiropractors, and otherwise honest consumers who do not regard insurance fraud as a "serious" crime all have been found to participate.

To combat insurance fraud, several states have created special fraud investigation bureaus within the states' insurance departments. Computerized fraud detection systems have proven highly successful in cracking fraud cases. And, increasingly, insurance companies are setting up special units of their own to investigate suspect claims.

The dilemma faced by every insurance company, says the National Association of Independent Insurers, is how to identify claims warranting an intensive investigation before settlement. Special investigative units staffed by fraud specialists, working with a company's claims department, are helping to solve that problem. While insurance industry experts note that insurance fraud probably cannot be prevented, most agree that special antifraud units can save insurance companies millions of dollars—costs that otherwise would be passed on to businesses and consumers.

Property Damaged by Arson in 1983

Property Classification	Number of Offenses	Average Monetary Value of Damage
STRUCTURES: TOTAL	51,690	$13,920
Single Occupancy		
Residential	24,371	9,418
Other Residential	8,064	10,119
Storage	5,154	16,308
Industrial/		
Manufacturing	825	59,372
Other Commercial	6,223	31,238
Community/Public	4,750	12,940
Other Structures	2,303	8,477
MOBILE VEHICLES:		
TOTAL	19,724	3,407
Motor Vehicles	17,992	2,938
Other Mobile Vehicles	1,732	8,280
OTHER: TOTAL	13,286	610
TOTAL	**84,700**	**9,384**

Source: *Crime in the United States*
U.S. Department of Justice
Federal Bureau of Investigation

As a result of recent industry and legislative actions, insurance policies have become more understandable to the layperson. Take the time to read and understand the policy you are investing in, address questions to the insurer, and insist on satisfactory answers. If you are concerned about the adequacy of a policy, consult your attorney or a legal firm specializing in insurance claims. Most insurance brokers, like any professional salesperson, will attempt to sell you the most comprehensive, and often the most expensive, policy. Legal counsel specializing in insurance coverage should be able to help to pare away any unnecessary coverage.

Fraudulent Claims

Perhaps the most effective way to reduce insurance losses due to employee or customer dishonesty is through a meticulous, knowledgeable examination of claims and potential fraud. Management should be on the alert for chronically ill employees who regularly file insurance or disability claims on the company policy, and should insist on the option of calling for a second medical opinion by a physician of the company's choice. Management and employees should also be alerted to customers who feign injuries while on company property; these customers should, if possible, be directed to a company or company-retained physician for examination. When customers or employees claim damage to personal property, local police and an attorney representing the company should be contacted immediately.

A report by the U.S. Chamber of Commerce lists the following "tip-offs" for false insurance claims.

- The person who "fell" or suffered an "accident" expresses a desire for an expeditious settlement.

- The claimant seems to have used exceptional dispatch in retaining an attorney.

- The claimant appears extraordinarily knowledgeable about the terminology and workings of the claim adjustment process.

- An injured claimant is treated at a hospital operated by his personal physician.

- The physician, despite repeated requests, fails to itemize bills.

- The injured parties are all treated by the same physician.

- The claimant uses a lawyer-physician combination that has been implicated in prior suspected frauds.

- Attempts to contact an employee claiming lost time due to an injury go unanswered.

 IF YOU ARE VICTIMIZED

Alleged false insurance claims by customers or employees and illegal practices by representatives of insurance companies should be brought to the immediate attention of your company attorney. Your attorney may advise you to contact local police, to refuse to honor an insurance claim, or to file a countersuit in court. In any case, since the recourse to insurance fraud almost always involves legal action, your response should be entrusted to a competent legal professional.

CHAPTER 17

The Systematic Stick-Up

After several years of trial and error and the formidable task of re-educating himself and his senior staff, the owner of an investment firm is finally satisfied that all company records and management functions have been successfully transferred to a highly efficient, cost-effective, in-house computer system.

The transformation required the owner and his staff to spend a considerable amount of time studying the computer's capabilities and operation procedures. A computer consultant was hired and had proven invaluable in assisting in setting up and explaining the new system of management and information storage and retrieval. For more than a year after the consultant left, the system had appeared to be working almost flawlessly. But now perplexing problems are beginning to occur.

Occasional discrepancies show up between the computer's financial printouts and the statements provided by the company's bank. Management has learned to place total faith in its new system and is certain the inaccuracies must be the result of bugs in the bank's computer system. Finally, the owner calls the company that

Computer Crime

sold him the computer equipment and requests that someone be assigned to work with the bank's computer personnel to clear up the problem.

A thorough review of the computer's records and programming activities uncovers the real culprit. Apparently, the computer consultant took advantage of his full access to the computer and its confidential contents to hide several lines of undocumented computer code in a program instructing the computer to disburse funds to a company which supposedly works for the investment firm. In reality, the funds are sent by the computer to a bank account opened under the consultant's name. Other codes alter financial records within the computer to camouflage the activities, circumventing built-in system safeguards. The conniving consultant also prudently entered undocumented codes that, when he accesses the computer over the phone lines, instructs it to issue an electronic warning if the system has been tampered with. Consequently, before the consultant can be sought for questioning, he has cleared his bank account of some $150,000 in fraudulently obtained funds, and disappeared.

Opening Pandora's Box

Computers are moving into the workplace at a speed virtually unprecedented by any other piece of business equipment. Not even the telephone, which in its advent revolutionized business communications, had so pervasive an impact on how business is conducted and managed.

Every day, hundreds of companies turn over many of the details of their management functions and controls to these high-tech tools. According to the International Data Corporation, by the end of 1985 American business will be equipped with some ten million personal computers, three out of four of which will be located in small and medium-sized businesses. And this figure does not include the nearly one hundred thousand mainframe computers already in place.

Few successes come without their price, and while these dramatic advancements may improve significantly the quality and cost-effectiveness of a company's services to clients, employees, and stockholders, they also lead to unprecedented opportunities for crime. For example, while the management of a newly computerized business enjoys access to more readily available information, it may also find that it has less direct control over vital business functions and less knowledge of the work supervised. A manager with limited understanding of computer operations may now have to supervise computer programmers, data entry clerks, and others placed in newly created positions of trust.

Perhaps even more potentially damaging is the concentration of massive amounts of vital, often confidential, information on small, easily transportable documents. "Floppy disks," for example, can contain the equivalent of hundreds of pages of information, yet they may be concealed between the pages of a magazine or destroyed with a lit cigarette or spilled cup of coffee.

Thus unprecedented technological advancements are matched by an equally unprecedented opportunity for crime. The theft of information—computer programs, marketing programs, customer lists, research and development data—has been estimated to cost as much as $20 billion a year, reports the National Institute of Justice. Increasingly, this information is stolen from a computer, in thefts that may be perpetrated in less than 0.003 second (3 milliseconds).

The Data Processing Management Association, which represents a large group of data processing managers, warns that business often unwittingly compounds the threat of crime. A 1984 Association survey revealed that only 65 percent of its data processing members had any budget for data security. This lack of concern for security, says an Association representative, is not unusual for managers new to the use of computers. All too often these neophytes act as if information stored inside a computer is automatically safe from intruders. Nothing could be further from the truth.

The Habits of the "Hacker"

Computer crime comes in many shapes. Input data can be altered to create fictitious accounts. Expensive computer time can be used for personal business. Fictitious payroll checks can be written and forged by computer. Confidential information can be obtained by tapping into a computer from a telephone hundreds, even thousands, of miles away. Sophisticated electronic devices, not directly connected to computer circuits, can be used to intercept information contained in the radiation generated by a computer's central processor.

Not all computer crime requires sophisticated equipment. An amateur computer enthusiast, or "hacker," equipped only with an inexpensive personal computer, a TV monitor, and a modem—a device that enables computer signals to be transmitted over telephone lines—can easily gain access to an unprotected computer network by phone and, intentionally or unwittingly, probe, alter, and even destroy some or all of the files in the computer's memory.

Most computer crimes fall into one of five categories, each category named for the primary source of the crime. Following are brief descriptions of crimes in the areas of programming activities, computer time, input data, output data, and data transfer.

1. **Programming activities.** A technically competent computer programmer enters specific instructions directing the computer to manipulate data. In the early 1980s, such cases included:

   - A disgruntled programmer who planted a "time bomb" that would have destroyed data in the computer's files three years after the programmer had left the company.

   - Another postdated programming instruction that would have instructed payroll to issue checks to a number of fictitious employees.

   - A programmer who so enjoyed travel that she built timed malfunctions into programs owned by clients around the U.S. This way she could plan on making frequent "working trips" to various parts of the country.

   Small companies, in which one employee often has sole responsibility for running the computer, are most vulnerable to this type of fraud. Large companies, by contrast, often have auditors who carefully monitor the activities of the programming and data entry staff.

The outright theft of programs also is becoming common-place. At a time when copyrighted off-the-shelf programs can cost thousands of dollars, determined hobbyists and software pirates are breaking through security codes to copy programs for subsequent personal use or sale. Dishonest employees, customers, and others with access to computer facilities may simply walk off with unguarded floppy disks that contain back-up or original programs.

2. **Computer time.** Whether it involves playing games on a com-pany-owned computer or operating a personal business using an employer's facilities, the unauthorized use of businesses' computer facilities is perhaps the most costly and pervasive computer crime.

    Much of this misuse takes place during nonpeak hours, such as lunch breaks or after 5 P.M., and while this type of crime is often linked to the misuse of a company's photocopier or office supplies, it can be far costlier and much harder to trace. In at least one known case, a business actually pur-chased a larger, more sophisticated computer system to ac-commodate what it assumed was a rapidly expanding business workload. In fact, the workload was expanding due to increased personal use of the easily accessible facilities.

3. **Input data.** Crimes involving input data encompass all decep-tive activities that manipulate, withhold, or fabricate data placed in the computer's memory for later use. Perhaps the simplest of these cons involves the withholding or outright destruction of information. For example, lists of a company's inventory may be destroyed, leaving the computer, and in turn management, in the dark when it comes to tracing inventory flow. This can allow the thief time to make off with a great deal of merchandise before inventory can be reviewed.

    Tampering with data can include the addition of names of fictitious suppliers to lists of approved vendors. Subsequent instructions might then authorize payments ostensibly made to the nonexistent suppliers that actually find their way into the programmer's pockets.

    As in programming crimes, small companies at which only one employee is responsible for computer activities are the most vulnerable to this form of internal fraud.

4. **Output data.** Perhaps the easiest and most directly damaging form of computer crime involves the theft of computer output. The thief simply steals what the computer produces, including printouts or punch cards of mailing lists or customer lists, and copyrighted, patented, or other confidential information.

There have been numerous cases of employees using stolen customer lists to start their own competitive businesses. Related cases have involved dishonest employees selling lists of current customer orders to competitive firms that may then approach these customers with a "better deal" on the same product or service.

5. **Data Transfer.** One of the true miracles of the computer revolution is the ability it confers of transporting virtual libraries of information over telephone lines in minutes or even seconds. Unfortunately, this miraculous capability also presents one of the weakest links in computer security.

   Data transfer over telephone lines normally takes place between a video display terminal and the company computer it is connected to, or between two separate computers exchanging information via a modem. Confidential information being transferred between two points can be intercepted via direct wiretaps, electromagnetic sensing devices that record radiation generated by the computer's central processor, or illegal entries into the information network. Illegal entries are accomplished by the use of unauthorized terminals that intercept signals transmitted by authorized terminals. The unauthorized terminal then instructs the computer network to remain open and allow the unauthorized user access to its contents. For this breach of security to take place, the system must be equipped with a telephone hook-up that enables the hacker to gain entry. Thus, this type of system is particularly vulnerable to outside threats.

   In a related offense, employees with access to a company's computer can make unauthorized transfers of data. For example, in one case, a bank teller transferred over $1 million to his personal account and then programmed the computer to destroy the evidence.

PROTECT YOUR BUSINESS

The vast majority of computer crimes are preventable. An effective deterrence system begins with an awareness on the part of the computer manager that computers can create myriad opportunities for crime. Just as a company's management takes the time to learn the skills necessary to participate in the operation of a new computer system, it should devote time to exploring and installing effective security measures.

Decisions about implementing a security system should be made *before* the system is installed. Experience has shown that during transition periods—those weeks or months during which a company transfers its manual systems of recordkeeping to a computer system—businesses are the most susceptible to computer crime. Therefore, crime watchers recommend that a well-planned, clear-cut security system be implemented from day one. As an added precaution during this transition period, companies are encouraged to continue their manual system of recordkeeping alongside the computer's recordkeeping. This overlapping should continue for at least two months, or for as long as it takes to remove the major "bugs" from the new system.

Install It, Enforce It

A company relying on the security of its computer system should develop and maintain a written and enforced security policy that addresses such issues as:

- **Employee hiring.** Thorough background checks on individuals being considered for key computer positions should include direct contacts with former employers, professional and personal references, verification of technical skills, and credit checks.

- **Access to computer facilities.** Only those employees whose work requires that they have access to computer facilities should be allowed in the computer area. Identities of repair personnel and technicians from outside the company should be verified by asking for identification and calling the company they represent. Also confirm that a service call was placed by someone with the authority to do so. A company employee should accompany the technician to the worksite, and a log book should be maintained with times and the names of all who have access to the computer facilities.

- **Physical security.** To ensure both safety and security, computer facilities should be located in relatively untrafficked areas. Ideally, equipment should be located in an isolated area containing adequate lighting, few windows or doors, a securely locking entrance, and, if possible, a security guard at each entrance. Guards should be required to check the identification of everyone requesting access to the facilities. Some companies provide employees with photo identification cards, others with cards containing fingerprints and/or codes that can be verified only by a deciphering machine at the computer facilities' entrance.

- **Functions and authority.** For security reasons, the computer processing department should be located physically apart from other departments. Employee functions and authority also should be separate, and no single employee should have control over an entire operation. The assignments of employees working in computer areas should be rotated on a regular basis.

- **Internal and external protective devices.** Management should take advantage of all available security devices that can be built into the computer system. The company that sells or leases the equipment can explain how passwords, security codes, and code scrambling devices can control access to the system. Electronic security devices, such as closed circuit television and sound-sensitive listening devices, also should be considered.

  Passwords allowing users to gain access to a computer should be a combination of six or more letters, numbers, and symbols and should not be words or figures that have a special significance to the computer owner, such as personal names or social security numbers. Employees should be instructed not to note passwords or other sensitive information on pieces of paper near the computer or in any nonsecured area, nor should such information be discussed during telephone or on-line conversations. Passwords should be changed periodically, and if there is any suspicion that security has been broken, they should be changed immediately.

  Computers can be programmed in a variety of ways to thwart would-be interlopers—by "stalling" after each wrong password is entered, disconnecting after a certain number of wrong guesses, recording attempts to penetrate, and even tracing a phone call after a certain number of unsuccessful attempts are made.

- **Storage procedures.** Programming materials and input and output data are only as safe as the storage system that contains them. Print-out bins, disk files, and tape libraries should be kept in an orderly fashion in an untrafficked area set aside solely for storage purposes. These areas, like all other computer areas, should be protected from water leakage and temperature variances. Ideally, there should be no windows and no more than two access doors in the storage area.

  Each document should be given a file number, which is recorded in a secure filing system, access to which is permitted only by written authorization from a specified member of management. The authorization should specify which documents are to be logged out and for what period of time, and documents removed from the storage area should be signed for on a carefully maintained daily register at the area's entrance.

The disposal of computer materials also should be treated with caution, with paper shredders or burning devices used to keep discarded information from falling into the wrong hands.

- **Periodic audits.** Both internal and independent audits of a company's records and security systems should be conducted at least once a year. This is especially crucial during the start-up phase of internal computer management.

  The auditors should have considerable experience in computer analysis and programming as well as in accounting practices. While auditors may be expected to closely scrutinize a company's recordkeeping systems, some of the more computer-wise auditing firms will attempt to defraud the company's system to determine whether security is sufficient.

 IF YOU ARE VICTIMIZED

Keeping in mind that some computer crimes are so sophisticated that they may take months, even years, to detect and unravel, management should be constantly on the alert for possible indications of wrongdoing. The most effective recourse begins with a willingness to investigate any and all questionable activities.

Confidential data somehow turns up in an area where it shouldn't be or comes up in conversation between persons who shouldn't have access to it; computer-generated data is found to be inconsistent with other business indicators; employees, customers, or suppliers complain about inaccurate computer-generated paperwork: any of these scenarios may be indicators of fraudulent activity.

If a company's investigation of an unusual business occurrence or security breach turns up the appearance of possible criminal activity, the local police department, local branch of the U.S. District Attorney's office, and the company's attorney should be contacted immediately. Legislation affecting computer crime is a complicated and changing area, with 21 states as of September 1984 enacting computer crime laws. These laws, for the most part, define computer crime and set various penalties for different types of criminal activity. In some states, however, the use of a computer for criminal activity may not in itself be a crime. In these cases, in order to prosecute a computer-related offense, it may be necessary to determine what property or services have been embezzled, stolen, misappropriated, or converted as a result of the computer manipulation, so that the suspect can be charged under the appropriate local, state, or federal law.

The federal government is also in the process of enacting federal laws and rules on the fraudulent use of computers. As of September 1984, Congress had passed a law directing the U.S. Small Business Administration to establish a security and education program to provide information on how to prevent computer crime. Congress is also considering several bills that would set federal penalties for the use of the computer for criminal activities.

The National Center for Computer Crime Data maintains up-to-date records on state laws on crime by computer. Copies of their publications may be obtained from the Center (See Appendix A).

Appendix A

The following list provides names and phone numbers for agencies and organizations referred to in this publication. The second column provides a quick sketch of the areas of activity of each organization as it relates to our topic. If you have questions about any service or agency in the federal government, the Federal Information Center nearest you (see page 179) can provide information and help you to locate the appropriate agency.

The names, addresses, phone numbers, and office descriptions presented here have been thoroughly checked. However, because of changes that may take place after publication, some information may no longer be current. We regret any inconvenience this may cause.

These agencies and organizations . . . . . . | **may provide answers and assistance in these areas**

Audit Bureau of Circulations
900 North Meacham Road
Schaumburg, IL 60173
(312) 885-0910

verifying newspaper circulation figures

Commodity Futures Trading
  Commission (CFTC)
2033 K Street, N.W.
Washington, D.C. 20581
(202) 254-6387

questions involving commodity futures trading and possible commodity futures fraud

Regional CFTC Offices

Chicago
   233 South Wacker Drive
   Suite 4600
   Chicago, IL 60606
   (312) 886-9000
Kansas City
   4901 Main Street
   Room 400
   Kansas City, MO 64112
   (816) 374-2131
Los Angeles
   10850 Wilshire Boulevard
   Suite 370
   Los Angeles, CA 90024
   (213) 209-6782

Minneapolis
   510 Grain Exchange Bldg.
   Minneapolis, MN 55415
   (612) 370-3255
New York
   One World Trade Center
   Suite 4747
   New York, NY 10048
   (212) 466-5723

Direct Selling Association
1776 K Street, N.W.
Suite 60
Washington, D.C. 20006
(202) 293-5760

questions involving door-to-door sales; verifying membership of companies involved in direct sales

Federal Bureau of
  Investigation
United States Department
  of Justice
Washington, D.C. 20535

all violations of federal law except those specifically assigned to other federal agencies

These agencies and organizations . . . . . . may provide answers and assistance in these areas

The FBI's field offices are located in major cities throughout the U.S. and in San Juan, Puerto Rico, and resident agencies (sub-offices) are maintained in smaller cities and towns in all parts of the country. The front page of most telephone directories lists the telephone number of the nearest FBI field office.

Federal Information Centers

Alabama
Birmingham (205) 322-8591
Mobile (205) 438-1421

Alaska
Anchorage (907) 271-3650

Arizona
Phoenix (602) 261-3313

Arkansas
Little Rock (501) 378-6177

California
Los Angeles (213) 894-3800
Sacramento (916) 551-2380
San Diego (619) 557-6030
San Francisco (415) 556-6600
Santa Ana (714) 836-2386

Colorado
Colorado Springs (303) 471-9491
Denver (303) 844-6575
Pueblo (303) 544-9523

Connecticut
Hartford (203) 527-2617
New Haven (203) 624-4720

Florida
Ft. Lauderdale (305) 522-8531
Jacksonville (904) 354-4756
Miami (305) 536-4155/4005
Orlando (305) 422-1800
St. Petersburg (813) 893-3495
Tampa (813) 229-7911
West Palm Beach (305) 883-7566

Hawaii
Honolulu (808) 541-1365

Illinois
Chicago (312) 353-4242

Indiana
Gary (219) 883-4110
Indianapolis (317) 269-7373

Iowa
From any Iowa location
800-532-1556 (toll free)

Kansas
From any Kansas location
1-800-432-2934 (toll free)

Kentucky
Louisville (502) 582-6261

Louisiana
New Orleans (504) 589-6696

Maryland
Baltimore (301) 962-4980

Massachusetts
Boston (617) 565-8121

Michigan
Detroit (313) 226-7016
Grand Rapids (616) 451-2628

Minnesota
Minneapolis (612) 370-3333

Missouri
St. Louis (314) 425-4106
From other Missouri locations
800-392-7711 (toll free)

Nebraska
Omaha (402) 221-3353
From other Nebraska locations
800-642-8383 (toll free)

New Jersey
Newark (201) 645-3600
Trenton (609) 396-4400

New Mexico
Albuquerque (505) 766-3091

New York
Albany (518) 463-4421
Buffalo (716) 846-4010
New York (212) 264-4464
Rochester (716) 546-5075
Syracuse (315) 476-8545

North Carolina
Charlotte (704) 376-3600

Ohio
Akron (216) 375-5638
Cincinnati (513) 684-2801
Cleveland (216) 522-4040
Columbus (614) 221-1014
Dayton (513) 223-7377
Toledo (419) 241-3223

Oklahoma
Oklahoma City (405) 231-4868
Tulsa (918) 584-4193

Oregon
Portland (503) 221-2222

Pennsylvania
Philadelphia (215) 597-7042
Pittsburgh (412) 644-INFO

Rhode Island
Providence (401) 521-5635

Tennessee
Chattanooga (615) 265-8231
Memphis (901) 521-3285
Nashville (615) 242-5056

Texas
Austin (512) 472-5494
Dallas (214) 767-8585
Fort Worth (817) 334-3624
Houston (713) 229-2552
San Antonio (512) 224-4471

Utah
Salt Lake City (801) 524-5353

Virginia
Norfolk (804) 441-3101
Richmond (804) 643-4928
Roanoke (703) 982-8591

Washington
Seattle (206) 442-0570
Tacoma (206) 383-5230

Wisconsin
Milwaukee (414) 271-2273

These agencies and organizations . . . . . .   may provide answers and assistance in these areas

Federal Trade Commission
  (FTC)
6th & Pennsylvania Ave., N.W.
Washington, D.C. 20580
(202) 326-3128

questions involving possible false advertising and other deceptive business practices

Regional FTC Offices

Atlanta
1718 Peachtree Street, N.W.
Suite 1000
Atlanta, GA 30367
(404) 347-4836

Boston
10 Causeway Street
Room 1184
Boston, MA 02222-1073
(617) 565-7240

Chicago
55 East Monroe Street
Suite 1437
Chicago, IL 60603
(312) 353-4423

Cleveland
118 St. Clair Avenue
Suite 500
The Mall Building
Cleveland, OH 44114
(216) 522-4207

Dallas
8303 Elmbrook Drive
Suite 140
Dallas, TX 75247
(214) 767-7053

Denver
1405 Curtis Street
Suite 2900
Denver, CO 80202
(303) 844-2271

Los Angeles
11000 Wilshire Boulevard
Los Angeles, CA 90024
(213) 209-7575

New York
26 Federal Plaza
22nd Floor
New York, NY 10278
(212) 264-1207

San Francisco
901 Market Street
Suite 570
San Francisco, CA 94103
(415) 995-5220

Seattle
915 Second Avenue
Federal Building
Room 2806
Seattle, WA 98174
(206) 442-4655/56

Fraud and Theft Information
  Bureau
Box 400
Boynton Beach, FL 33425
(305) 737-7500

information on prevention techniques for credit card and check fraud

Internal Revenue Service
Director EP/EO
Operations Division
1111 Constitution Avenue, N.W.
E:O Room 2557
Washington, D.C. 20224
(202) 566-4311

filing a complaint against a deceptive charitable soliciting organization

National Center for
  Computer Crime Data
2700 North Cahuenga Boulevard
Suite 2113
Los Angeles, CA 90068
(213) 874-8233

current information on legislation concerning computer crime

National Futures Association
200 West Madison Street
Suite 1600
Chicago, IL 60606
(312) 781-1300

questions involving commodity future sales; verifying membership of company involved in commodity sales

These agencies and organizations . . . . . .

may provide answers and assistance in these areas

Securities and Exchange
  Commission (SEC)
Office of Consumer Affairs
  Information Services
450 5th Street, N.W.
Washington, D.C. 20549
(202) 272-7440

questions about securities dealings; verifying registration of
securities brokers and their firms

Regional SEC Offices

Atlanta
  Suite 788
  1375 Peachtree Street, N.E.
  Atlanta, GA 30367
  (404) 347-4768

Boston
  J.W. McCormick Post Office and
    Court House Building
  Suite 700
  Boston, MA 02109
  (617) 223-9900

Chicago
  Room 1204
  Everett McKinley Dirksen Bldg.
  219 South Dearborn Street
  Chicago, IL 60604
  (312) 353-7390

Denver
  Suite 700
  410 Seventeenth Street
  Denver, CO 80202
  (303) 844-2071

Fort Worth
  8th Floor
  411 West Seventh Street
  Fort Worth, TX 76102
  (817) 334-3821

Los Angeles
  5757 Wilshire Boulevard
  Suite 500 East
  Los Angeles, CA 90036-3648
  (213) 468-3107

New York
  Room 1102
  26 Federal Plaza
  New York, NY 10278
  (212) 264-1636

Seattle
  3040 Jackson Federal Building
  915 Second Avenue
  Seattle, WA 98174
  (206) 442-7990

Washington
  Public Reference Branch
  450 5th Street, N.W.
  Washington, D.C. 20549
  (202) 272-7450

U.S. Copyright Office
Library of Congress
Washington, D.C. 20559
(202) 479-0700

registering copyrights

U.S. Customs Service
Department of the Treasury
1301 Constitution Avenue, N.W.
Washington, D.C. 20229
(202) 566-8157

recording registered trademarks and copyrights

U.S. Patent and Trademark Office
2011 Jefferson Davis Highway
Crystal Plaza, #2
Arlington, VA 22202
(703) 557-3158

registering trademarks, obtaining a list of registered patent
attorneys in a specific geographic area

Chief Postal Inspector
Fraud Section
U.S. Postal Service
475 L'Enfant Plaza West, S.W.
Washington, D.C. 20260
(202) 268-4299

reporting violations of federal postal laws, including phony
invoices, solicitations disguised as invoices, and any scheme
that includes documents sent through the U.S. mail

Appendix B

The Council of Better Business Bureaus is a business-supported nonprofit organization devoted to the protection of the consuming public and the vitality of the free enterprise system. Serving as the national headquarters for the 174 local Better Business Bureaus, the Council promotes truth in advertising, resolves consumer/business disputes, develops industry standards for advertising and sales, and conducts consumer information programs.

The Philanthropic Advisory Service, a division of the Council, monitors and reports on national soliciting organizations and conducts counseling and educational activities to aid both contributors and nonprofit groups.

COUNCIL OF BETTER
  BUSINESS BUREAUS, INC.
1515 Wilson Blvd.
Arlington, VA 22209
(703) 276-0100

PHILANTHROPIC ADVISORY SERVICE
Council of Better Business Bureaus, Inc.
1515 Wilson Blvd.
Arlington, VA 22209
(703) 276-0100

Local Bureaus

ALABAMA
THE BBB, INC.
P.O. Box 55268
1214 S. 20th Street
Birmingham, AL 35205
(205) 933-2893

BBB OF NORTH
  ALABAMA, INC.
501 Church Street, NW
Huntsville, AL 35801
(205) 533-1640

BBB OF SOUTH
  ALABAMA, INC.
707 Van Antwerp Building
Mobile, AL 36602
(205) 433-5494, 95

The Better Business
  Bureau, Inc.
Union Bank Building
Commerce Street
Suite 810
Montgomery, AL 36104
(205) 262-5606

ALASKA
BBB OF ALASKA, INC.
3380 C Street
Suite 100
Anchorage, AK 99503
(907) 562-0704

ARIZONA
BBB OF MARICOPA
  COUNTY, INC.
4428 North 12th Street
Phoenix, AZ 85014
(602) 264-1721

BBB OF TUCSON, INC.
50 W. Drachman Street
Suite 103
Tucson, AZ 85705
(602) 622-7651

ARKANSAS
BBB OF ARKANSAS, INC.
1216 South University Avenue
Little Rock, AR 72204
(501) 664-7274

CALIFORNIA
BBB OF SOUTH CENTRAL
  CALIFORNIA, INC.
705 Eighteenth Street
Bakersfield, CA 93301-4882
(805) 322-2074

BBB OF INLAND CITIES
290 N. 10th Street, Suite 206
P.O. Box 970
Colton, CA 92324-0522
(714) 825-7280

BBB OF CENTRAL
  CALIFORNIA, INC.
5070 North Sixth, Suite 176
Fresno, CA 93710
(209) 222-8111

BBB OF MONTEREY, INC.
301 Webster Street, Suite 305
Monterey, CA 93940
(408) 372-3149

BBB, INC.
510 16th Street, Suite 550
Oakland, CA 94612
(415) 839-5900

SACRAMENTO VALLEY BBB
400 S Street
Sacramento, CA 95814
(916) 443-6843

BBB OF SAN DIEGO, LTD.
Union Bank Building, Suite 301
525 B Street
San Diego, CA 92101-4408
(619) 234-0966

BBB OF SAN FRANCISCO
33 New Montgomery St. Tower
San Francisco, CA 94105
(415) 243-9999

BBB OF SANTA CLARA
VALLEY, LTD.
1505 Meridian Avenue
San Jose, CA 95125
(408) 978-8700

BBB OF SAN MATEO
COUNTY, INC.
P.O. Box 294
20 North San Mateo Drive
San Mateo, CA 94401
(415) 347-1251

BBB OF TRI-COUNTIES
P.O. Box 746
111 No. Milpas Street
Santa Barbara, CA 93102
(805) 963-8657

BBB OF MID COUNTIES, INC.
1111 North Center Street
Stockton, CA 95202
(209) 948-4880, 81

COLORADO
BBB OF THE PIKES PEAK
REGION, INC.
3022 N. El Paso
Colorado Springs, CO 80907
(303) 636-1155

ROCKY MOUNTAIN BBB, INC.
1780 South Bellaire, Suite 700
Denver, CO 80222
(303) 758-8200

BBB OF NORTHERN
COLORADO, INC.
140 West Oak Street
Fort Collins, CO 80524
(303) 484-1348

BBB OF SOUTHERN
COLORADO, INC.
432 Broadway & Grant
Pueblo, CO 81004
(303) 542-6464

CONNECTICUT
BBB OF WESTERN
CONNECTICUT, INC.
Fairfield Woods Plaza
P.O. Box 1410
2345 Black Rock Turnpike
Fairfield, CT 06430
(203) 374-6161

BBB OF NORTHERN
CONNECTICUT, INC.
630 Oakwood Avenue
Suite 223
West Hartford, CT 06110
(203) 247-8700

BBB OF SE
CONNECTICUT, INC.
100 S. Turnpike Road
Wallingford, CT 06492
(203) 269-2700, 269-4457

DELAWARE
KENT SUSSEX BBB, INC.
20 South Walnut Street
P.O. Box 300
Milford, DE 19963
(302) 422-6300 (Kent)
(302) 856-6969 (Sussex)

BBB OF DELAWARE, INC.
2055 Limestone Road
Suite 200
P.O. Box 5361
Wilmington, DE 19808
(302) 996-9200

DISTRICT OF COLUMBIA
BBB OF METROPOLITAN
WASHINGTON
1012 14th Street, NW -
14th Floor
Washington , D.C. 20005
(202) 393-8000

FLORIDA
BBB OF WEST FLORIDA, INC.
13770 58th Street, N
Suite 309
Clearwater, FL 33520
(813) 535-5522
Sarasota & Manatee
(813) 957-0093

BBB OF SOUTH FLORIDA, INC.
Lee/Collier Division
3089 Cleveland Avenue
P.O. Box 2155
Fort Myers, FL 33902
(813) 334-7331, 7152

BBB OF NORTHEAST
FLORIDA, INC.
3100 University Boulevard, South
Suite 239
Jacksonville, FL 32216
(904) 721-2288

BBB OF SOUTH FLORIDA, INC.
16291 Northwest 57th Avenue
Miami, FL 33014-6709
(305) 625-0307

BBB OF CENTRAL
FLORIDA, INC.
132 E. Colonial Drive
Suite 213
Orlando, FL 32801
(305) 843-8873

BBB OF NORTHWEST
FLORIDA, INC.
P.O. Box 1511
Pensacola, FL 32597-1511
(904) 433-6111

BBB OF PALM BEACH,
MARTIN & ST. LUCIE
COUNTIES
3015 Exchange Court
West Palm Beach, FL 33409
(305) 686-2200

GEORGIA
BBB OF METROPOLITAN
ATLANTA, INC.
100 Edgewood Avenue
Suite 1012
Atlanta, GA 30303
(404) 688-4910

BBB OF AUGUSTA, INC.
624 Ellis Street
Suite 106
Augusta, GA 30901
(404) 722-1574

BBB OF WEST GEORGIA-
EAST ALABAMA, INC.
Eight 13th Street
P.O. Box 2587
Columbus, GA 31902
(404) 324-0712, 13

BBB OF THE COASTAL
EMPIRE, INC.
6822 Abercorn Street
P.O. Box 13956
Savannah, GA 31416-0956
(912) 354-7521

HAWAII
BBB OF HAWAII, INC.
1600 Kapiolani Blvd., Suite 714
Honolulu, HI 96814
(808) 942-2355

IDAHO
BBB OF TREASURE
VALLEY, INC.
409 W. Jefferson
Boise, ID 83702
(208) 342-4649

BBB OF EASTERN
  IDAHO, INC.
545 Shoup — Suite 239
Idaho Falls, ID 83402
(208) 523-9754

ILLINOIS

BBB OF CHICAGO &
  NORTHERN ILLINOIS, INC.
211 West Wacker Drive
Chicago, IL 60601
(312) 444-1188

BBB OF CENTRAL
  ILLINOIS, INC.
109 S.W. Jefferson Street
Suite 305
Peoria, IL 61602
(309) 673-5194

INDIANA

BBB OF ELKHART
  COUNTY, INC.
118 South Second Street
P.O. Box 405
Elkhart, IN 46515
(219) 293-5731

EVANSVILLE REGIONAL BBB
119 S.E. Fourth Street
Evansville, IN 47708
(812) 422-6879

BBB OF NORTHEASTERN
  INDIANA, INC.
1203 Webster Street
Fort Wayne, IN 46802
(219) 423-4433

BBB OF NORTHWEST
  INDIANA, INC.
4231 Cleveland Street
Gary, IN 46408
(219) 980-1511

CENTRAL INDIANA BBB, INC.
Victoria Centre
22 E. Washington Street
Suite 310
Indianapolis, IN 46204
(317) 637-0197

BBB OF NORTHEASTERN
  INDIANA, INC.
204 Iroquois Building
Marion, IN 46952
(317) 668-8954, 55

BALL STATE UNIVERSITY BBB
Whitinger Building — Room 160
P.O. Box 192
Muncie, IN 47306
(317) 285-5668

BBB OF MICHIANA, INC.
50985 US #33, North
South Bend, IN 46637
(219) 277-9121

IOWA

BBB/QUAD CITIES
Alpine Centre
2435 Kimberly Road
Suite 110-N
Bettendorf, IA 52722
(319) 355-6344

CEDAR RAPIDS AREA BBB
1500 Second Avenue, S.E.
Suite 212
Cedar Rapids, IA 52403
(319) 366-5401

BBB OF CENTRAL &
  EASTERN IOWA
615 Insurance Exchange Bldg.
Des Moines, IA 50309
(515) 243-8137

BBB OF SIOUXLAND, INC.
318 Badgerow Building
Sioux City, IA 51101
(712) 252-4501

KANSAS

BBB OF NORTHEAST
  KANSAS, INC.
501 Jefferson — Suite 24
Topeka, KS 66607
(913) 232-0455

BBB, INC.
300 Kaufman Building
Wichita, KS 67202
(316) 263-3146

KENTUCKY

BBB OF CENTRAL
  KENTUCKY, INC.
154 Patchen Dr., Suite 90
Lexington, KY 40502
(606) 268-4128

THE BBB, INC.
844 South 4th Street
Louisville, KY 40203
(502) 583-6546

LOUISIANA

BBB ALEXANDRIA-PINEVILLE
1407 Murray Street
Suite 101
Alexandria, LA 71301
(318) 473-4494

BBB OF SOUTH CENTRAL
  LA, INC.
2055 Wooddale Blvd.
Baton Rouge, LA 70806
(504) 926-3010

BBB-TRI PARISH AREA
300 Bond Street
Houma, LA 70361
(504) 868-3456

BBB OF ACADIANA, INC.
100 Huggins Road
P.O. Box 30297
Lafayette, LA 70593
(318) 981-3497

BBB OF SOUTHWEST
  LOUISIANA, INC.
1413-C Ryan Street
P.O. Box 1681
Lake Charles, LA 70602
(318) 433-1633

BBB OF NORTHEAST
  LOUISIANA, INC.
141 De Siard Street
Suite 300
Monroe, LA 71201
(318) 387-4600, 01

BBB OF GREATER
  NEW ORLEANS AREA, INC.
301 Camp Street — Suite 403
New Orleans, LA 70130
(504) 581-6222

THE BBB
1401 North Market Street
Shreveport, LA 71107
(318) 221-8352

MAINE

BBB OF MAINE, INC.
812 Stevens Avenue
Portland, ME 04103
(207) 878-2715

MARYLAND

BBB OF GREATER
  MARYLAND, INC.
401 North Howard Street
Baltimore, MD 21201
(301) 347-3990

MASSACHUSETTS

THE BBB, INC.
8 Winter Street — 6th Floor
Boston, MA 02108
(617) 482-9151

BBB OF METRO WEST
One Kendall Street
Suite 307
Framingham, MA 01701
(617) 872-5585

BBB OF CAPE COD &
  THE ISLANDS
78 North Street — Suite 1
Hyannis, MA 02501
(617) 771-3022

BBB OF MERRIMACK VALLEY
316 Essex Street
Lawrence, MA 01840
(617) 687-7666

BBB OF SE
  MASSACHUSETTS, INC.
106 State Road — Suite 4
North Dartmouth, MA 02747
(617) 999-6060

BBB OF WESTERN
MASSACHUSETTS, INC.
293 Bridge Street — Suite 324
Springfield, MA 01103
(413) 734-3114

BBB OF CENTRAL
NEW ENGLAND, INC.
32 Franklin Street
P.O. Box 379
Worcester, MA 01601
(617) 755-2548

MICHIGAN
BBB OF DETROIT &
E. MICHIGAN, INC.
150 Michigan Avenue
Detroit, MI 48226-2646
(313) 962-7566

BBB OF WESTERN
MICHIGAN, INC.
620 Trust Building
Grand Rapids, MI 49503
(616) 774-8236

MINNESOTA
BBB OF MINNESOTA
1745 University Avenue
St. Paul, MN 55104
(612) 646-4631

MISSISSIPPI
BBB OF MISSISSIPPI/
Biloxi Branch
2917 W. Beach Blvd.
Suite 103
Biloxi, MS 39531
(601) 374-2222

BBB OF MISSISSIPPI/
Columbus Branch
105 Fifth Street
Columbus, MS 39701
(601) 327-8594

BBB OF MISSISSIPPI/
Hattiesburg Branch
1201 W. Pine Street, Suite 4
Hattiesburg, MS 39401
(601) 582-0116

BBB OF MISSISSIPPI, INC.
501 George Street — Suite 107
P.O. Box 2090
Jackson, MS 39225-2090
(601) 948-8222

BBB OF MISSISSIPPI/
Meridian Branch
P.O. Box 5512
Meridian, MS 39302
(601) 482-8752

MISSOURI
BBB OF GREATER
KANSAS CITY, INC.
306 East 12th Street
Suite 1024
Kansas City, MO 64106
(816) 421-7800

BBB OF E. MISSOURI &
SO. ILLINOIS
5100 Oakland, Suite 200
St. Louis, MO 63110
(314) 531-3300

BBB OF SOUTHWEST
MISSOURI, INC.
205 Park Central East
Suite 509
P.O. Box 4331 GS
Springfield, MO 65806
(417) 862-9231

NEBRASKA
CORNHUSKER BBB, INC.
719 North 48th Street
Lincoln, NE 68504
(402) 467-5261

BBB OF OMAHA, INC.
1613 Farnam Street, Room 417
Omaha, NE 68102
(402) 346-3033

NEVADA
BBB OF SOUTHERN
NEVADA, INC.
1022 E. Sahara Avenue
Las Vegas, NV 89104
(702) 735-6900

BBB OF NORTHERN
NEVADA, INC.
372-A Casazza Drive
P.O. Box 2932
Reno, NV 89505
(702) 322-0657

NEW HAMPSHIRE
BBB OF GRANITE STATE
One Pillsbury Street
Concord, NH 03301
(603) 224-1991

NEW JERSEY
BBB OF GREATER
NEWARK, INC.
34 Park Place
Newark, NJ 07102
(201) 643-3025

BBB OF BERGEN, PASSAIC &
ROCKLAND COUNTIES
2 Forest Avenue
Paramus, NJ 07652
(201) 845-4044

OCEAN COUNTY BBB
1721 Route 37 East
Toms River, NJ 08753
(201) 270-5577

BBB OF CENTRAL
NEW JERSEY, INC.
1700 Whitehorse
Hamilton Square, Suite D-5
Trenton, NJ 08690
Mercer County
(609) 588-0808
Monmouth County
(201) 536-6306
Middlesex, Somerset &
Hunderton Counties
(201) 329-6855

BBB OF SOUTH JERSEY, INC.
16 Maple Avenue
P.O. Box 303
Westmont, NJ 08108-0303
(609) 854-8467

NEW MEXICO
BBB OF NEW MEXICO, INC.
4600-A Montgomery, N.E.
Suite 200
Albuquerque, NM 87109
(505) 884-0500

BBB/FOUR CORNERS, INC.
308 North Locke
Farmington, NM 87401
(505) 326-6501

BBB OF SANTA FE
1210 Luisa Street
Suite 5
Santa Fe, NM 87502
(505) 988-3648

NEW YORK
BBB OF WESTERN
NEW YORK, INC.
775 Main Street
Suite 401
Buffalo, NY 14203
(716) 856-7180

LONG ISLAND BBB
266 Main Street
Farmingdale, NY 11735
(516) 420-0500

BBB OF METROPOLITAN
NEW YORK, INC.
257 Park Avenue South
New York, NY 10010
(212) 533-6200

BBB OF ROCHESTER, INC.
1122 Sibley Tower
Rochester, NY 14604
(716) 546-6776

BBB, INC. SERVING CENTRAL
NY, THE NORTH COUNTRY &
THE SOUTHERN TIER
100 University Building
Syracuse, NY 13202
(315) 479-6635

BBB OF THE MOHAWK
VALLEY, INC.
258 Genesee Street
Utica, NY 13502
(315) 724-3129

BBB OF WESTCHESTER,
PUTNAM AND DUCHESS
COUNTIES
One Brockway Place
White Plains, NY 10601
(914) 428-1230, 31
120 E. Main Street
Wappingers Falls, NY 12590
(914) 297-6550

NORTH CAROLINA
THE BBB OF ASHEVILLE/
WESTERN NORTH
CAROLINA, INC.
29½ Page Avenue
Asheville, NC 28801
(704) 253-2392

THE BBB OF THE SOUTHERN
PIEDMONT, INC.
1130 East 3rd Street, Suite 400
Charlotte, NC 28204
(704) 332-7151

BBB OF CENTRAL NORTH
CAROLINA, INC.
3608 West Friendly Avenue
Greensboro, NC 27410
(919) 852-4240, 41, 42

BBB OF CATAWBA COUNTY
P.O. Box 1882
Hickory, NC 28603
(704) 464-0372

BBB OF EASTERN NORTH
CAROLINA, INC.
3120 Poplarwood Drive
Suite G-1
Raleigh, NC 27604
(919) 872-9240

THE BBB, INC.
2110 Cloverdale Avenue
Suite 2-B
Winston-Salem, NC 27103
(919) 725-8348

OHIO
BBB OF AKRON, INC.
137 South Main Street
Suite 200
P.O. Box 596
Akron, OH 44308
(216) 253-4590

BBB OF STARK COUNTY, INC.
1434 Cleveland Avenue, NW
Canton, OH 44703
(216) 454-9401

CINCINNATI BBB, INC.
898 Walnut Street
Cincinnati, OH 45202
(513) 421-3015

THE BBB, INC.
2217 East 9th Street
Cleveland, OH 44115
(216) 241-7678

BBB OF CENTRAL OHIO, INC.
527 South High Street
Columbus, OH 43215
(614) 221-6336

BBB OF DAYTON/
MIAMI VALLEY, INC.
40 West Fourth Street
Suite 280
Dayton, OH 45402
(513) 222-5825

MANSFIELD AREA BBB
130 W. 2nd Street
P.O. Box 1706
Mansfield, OH 44901
(419) 522-1700

BBB SERVING NW OHIO &
SE MICHIGAN, INC.
425 Jefferson Avenue
Suite 909
Toledo, OH 43604-1055
(419) 241-6276

WOOSTER AREA BBB
345 N. Market
Wooster, OH 44691
(216) 263-6444

BBB OF MAHONING
VALLEY, INC.
311 Mahoning Bank Building
P.O. Box 1495
Youngstown, OH 44501
(216) 744-3111

OKLAHOMA
BBB OF CENTRAL
OKLAHOMA, INC.
17 S. Dewey
Oklahoma City, OK 73102
(405) 239-6084

BBB OF TULSA, INC.
4833 South Sheridan
Suite 412
Tulsa, OK 74145
(918) 664-1266

OREGON
PORTLAND BBB, INC.
520 SW Sixth Avenue
Suite 600
Portland, OR 97204
(503) 226-3981

PENNSYLVANIA
LEIGH VALLEY BBB OF
EASTERN PA
528 North New Street
Bethlehem, PA 18018
(215) 866-8780

CAPITAL DIVISION OF BBB
OF EASTERN PA
53 North Duke Street
Lancaster, PA 17602
(717) 291-1151

BBB OF EASTERN
PENNSYLVANIA
1930 Chestnut Street
P.O. Box 2297
Philadelphia, PA 19103
(215) 496-1000

BBB OF WESTERN
PENNSYLVANIA, INC.
610 Smithfield Street
Pittsburgh, PA 15222
(412) 456-2700

BBB OF NORTHEASTERN
PA, INC.
601 Connell Building-6th Floor
P.O. Box 993
Scranton, PA 18501
(717) 342-9129

PUERTO RICO
BBB OF PUERTO RICO, INC.
GPO Box 70212
San Juan, PR 00936
(809) 756-5400

RHODE ISLAND
BBB OF RHODE ISLAND, INC.
270 Weybosset Street
Providence, RI 02903
(401) 272-9800

SOUTH CAROLINA
BBB OF THE MIDLANDS
1830 Bull Street
Columbia, SC 29201
(803) 254-2525

BBB OF THE FOOTHILLS
311 Pettigru Street
Greenville, SC 29601
(803) 242-5052

BBB OF COASTAL
CAROLINA, INC.
831 Flatiron Bldg., Suite 12
Highway #17, North
Myrtle Beach, SC 29577
(803) 448-6100

TENNESSEE
BBB, INC.
Park Plaza Building
1010 Market Street—Suite 200
Chattanooga, TN 37402
(615) 266-6144

BBB OF GREATER
EAST TENNESSEE, INC.
900 East Hill Avenue, Suite 165
P.O. Box 10327
Knoxville, TN 37939-0327
(615) 522-1300

MEMPHIS AREA BBB, INC.
1835 Union — Suite 312
P.O. Box 41406
Memphis, TN 38174-1406
(901) 272-9641

BBB OF NASHVILLE/MIDDLE
TENNESSEE, INC.
506 Nashville City Bank Bldg.
Nashville, TN 37201
(615) 254-5872

TEXAS

BBB OF ABILENE, INC.
Bank of Commerce Building
Suite 320
P.O. Box 3275
Abilene, TX 79604
(915) 691-1533

BBB OF THE
GOLDEN SPREAD
1008 W. 10th
P.O. Box 1905
Amarillo, TX 79105
(806) 374-3735

THE BBB, INC.
1005 MBank Plaza
Austin, TX 78701
(512) 476-6943

BBB OF SOUTHEAST
TEXAS, INC.
476 Oakland Avenue
P.O. Box 2988
Beaumont, TX 77704
(409) 835-5348

BBB OF BRAZOS
VALLEY, INC.
202 Varisco Building
Bryan, TX 77803
(409) 823-8148, 49

BBB OF THE COASTAL
BEND, INC.
109 N. Chaparral — Suite 101
Corpus Christi, TX 78401
(512) 888-5555

BBB OF METRO
DALLAS, INC.
2001 Bryan Street — Suite 850
Dallas, TX 75201
(214) 220-2000

BBB OF PASO DEL
NORTE, INC.
6024 Gateway East
Suite 1-C
El Paso, TX 79905-2096
(915) 778-7000

BBB AT FORT WORTH
SERVING TARRANT,
JOHNSON, HOOD, WISE,
PARKER & PALO PINTO
COUNTIES, INC.
709 Sinclair Building
106 West 5th Street
Fort Worth, TX 76102
(817) 332-7585

BBB OF METROPOLITAN
HOUSTON, INC.
2707 North Loop West
Suite 900
Houston, TX 77008
(713) 868-9500

BBB OF THE SOUTH
PLAINS, INC.
1015 15th Street
P.O. Box 1178
Lubbock, TX 79408
(806) 763-0459

BBB OF THE PERMIAN
BASIN, INC.
Airport Road 20
P.O. Box 6006
Midland, TX 79711
(915) 563-1880

BBB OF SAN ANGELO, INC.
1207 S. Bryant
P.O. Box 3366
San Angelo, TX 76902-3366
(915) 653-2318

THE BETTER BUSINESS
BUREAU
1800 Northeast Loop 410
Suite 400
San Antonio, TX 78217
(512) 828-9441

BBB OF CENTRAL EAST
TEXAS, INC.
3502-D South Broadway
P.O. Box 6652
Tyler, TX 75711-6652
(214) 581-5704

BBB OF WACO, INC.
6801 Sanger Avenue
Suite 125
P.O. Box 7203
Waco, TX 76714-7203
(817) 772-7530

BBB OF SOUTH TEXAS, INC.
P.O. Box 69
Weslaco, TX 78596-0069
(512) 968-3678

BBB OF NORTH CENTRAL
TEXAS, INC.
1106 Brook Street
Wichita Falls, TX 76301-5009
(817) 723-5526

UTAH

THE BBB, INC.
385 - 24th Street - Suite 717
Ogden, UT 84401
(801) 399-4701

BBB OF UTAH
1588 South Main Street
Salt Lake City, UT 84115
(801) 487-4656

VIRGINIA

BBB OF GREATER HAMPTON
ROADS, INC.
3608 Tidewater Drive
Norfolk, VA 23509
(804) 627-5651

BBB OF CENTRAL
VIRGINIA, INC.
701 East Franklin — Suite 712
Richmond, VA 23219
(804) 648-0016

BBB OF WESTERN
VIRGINIA, INC.
121 West Campbell Avenue
Roanoke, VA 24011-1290
(703) 342-3455

WASHINGTON

TRI-CITY BBB, INC.
127 W. Canal Drive
Kennewick, WA 99336
(509) 582-0222

BETTER BUSINESS BUREAU
2401 Bristol Court
Olympia, WA 98502
(206) 754-4254

BBB OF GREATER
SEATTLE, INC.
828 Denny Building
2200 Sixth Avenue
Seattle, WA 98121
(206) 448-8888

BETTER BUSINESS BUREAU
South 176 Stevens
Spokane, WA 99204
(509) 747-1155

THE BBB, INC.
1101 Fawcett Avenue #222
P.O. Box 1274
Tacoma, WA 98401
(206) 383-5561

BBB OF CENTRAL
WASHINGTON, INC.
418 Washington Mutual Building
P.O. Box 1584
Yakima, WA 98907
(509) 248-1326

WISCONSIN

BBB OF GREATER
MILWAUKEE
740 North Plankinton Avenue
Milwaukee, WI 53203
(414) 273-1600

Index